Your Guide to Lighthearted

EMBODY FIERCE JOY

Ancient Secrets to Transform Approval-Seeking into Supernatural Boldness

MARGUERITE BACA

Creator of the classic – Buns of Steel Yoga

ISBN: 979-8-89316-161-8 - hardcover
ISBN: 979-8-89316-162-5 - paperback
ISBN: 979-8-89316-163-2 - ebook

My Mom

When I was a little girl she embarrassed me by always being the first one on the dance floor, enjoying herself like nobody was watching. Now, I'm very much my mother's daughter, enjoying the countless gifts of life, including dancing. I'm in awe of your ability to embody fierce joy through all of life's circumstances, no matter how challenging. You taught us the power of words, and our minds, for maintaining health. Thank you for always encouraging our individual creative expression.

My Dad

You told me I could be anything I want to be, and I believed you. That bold confidence has led me to fulfill dreams beyond my wildest imagination. You gave us a great balance of spiritual devotion, discipline, and fun. Thank you for your playful humor, and most of all, for teaching me the power of prayer and faith.

My Brother

I scored growing up with my best friend, who is also my brother! I loved growing up with you and still do. This book would not have been written without your steadfast loyalty, support, and belief in me. Your spiritual faith and love of all people inspires me every day. I love you for eternity!

In Loving Memory Ruth Anne May
January 5, 1940 – March 27, 2024
My Spiritual Mama from the Village

Acknowledgment

Writing this book has transformed me in rewarding ways, far beyond my imagination. I am so thankful to everyone who has provided guidance, inspiration, and support for writing my first book. I give thanks to Jesus Christ, Paramahansa Yogananda, all the great masters, teachers, guiding influences, and celestial beings that have been present with me all my life. I am grateful for the priceless spiritual guidance, laughter, and steady support from my dear friend, Reverend Emma Molina-Ynequez, who cheers me on through all my various "stages" of life. Deepest heart-felt gratitude to my editor, Michael Jarnebro, who immediately understood me and my quirky ways. I could not have felt safer sharing my words, ideas, and voice. During our joyful collaboration, I became more fully me.

Contents

Preface

How Comfortable Are You in Your Own Skin?

The painfully shy person I used to be is now like a foggy, sad memory. She cringed with nervousness and broke out into a visible dripping sweat at the thought of simply raising her hand to speak, all this, before even uttering a word. When she was called upon to share, her face flushed with redness; her voice quivered uncontrollably along with her shaky hands. She had mistaken humbleness with diminishing her accomplishments, gifts, and powers. Sometimes she sacrificed her dignity, even her health, to fit in, to belong, to receive approval.

Not anymore. I'm done with that now.

In my journey to developing confidence, the mini transformations, consistent efforts, and progress have led me to become so bold that I even became a stand-up comedian. Quite frequently I am told, "You're so comfortable in your own skin, unapologetically you." It's true. I am.

This book is filled with lighthearted wisdom for serious-ass issues, wisdom I've gleaned from facing life's beautiful lessons. By putting some daily effort into the Ancient Secrets, you will also develop trust in yourself and embody fierce joy. It's a matter of health! I've gone from approval-seeking addict to awareness junkie. For me, nothing else tops the feelings of ease that come from that greater light of awareness, truth, and understanding. The eternal treasure of awareness has given me the ultimate freedom of not giving a flying hoot about anybody else's opinion of me and to trust my Joy Source.

Imagine the freedom of being immune to the incessant bombardment of opinions, limiting projections, and erroneous assumptions that people hurl at each other. The Secrets in this book will assist you in penetrating through the noise of the world to *your* steady Joy Source and the fun of fulfilling *your* soulful visions.

I've even come to find my own opinions to be downright boring compared to the realm of creativity and inspiration, which the Secrets open you to. You will also be able to conquer approval addiction and find the fun of transforming chaos into calmness. Calmness is the foundation of connecting to your Joy Source. Eventually, you will even begin to sense others' chaos and prevent it from touching your personal world. Isn't that ironic, that mastering calmness can be an exciting thrill?

The Secrets guide you, from your deepest knowing to the actions or nonactions that will not only prevent resentment buildup but also keep you safe and healthy and increase your tenderness capacity. Consider this your joy training manual for making the mystical practical, for becoming adept at listening to your intuition, the all-knowing faculty of your soul. You will gain calm knowing of what your heart and soul are calling you to do while remaining free of internal and external joy robbers.

Your journey began at conception when the first system of your body developed, the nervous system, including the formation of your brain. These are the two channels where the pure substance of life, pure joy, first entered your embryonic form. With the Secrets you will learn to masterfully return to your Joy Source and will get hooked on that pure substance of life. By depending on the steadiness and beauty of this source, you will free yourself from approval-seeking and become a downright awareness junkie!

At a bare minimum, the Secrets are healthy coping mechanisms for managing anxiety and enabling you to face challenges. As you increase your dependence on this priceless inner resource, the temptation to slip into numbing substance abuse and other compulsions begins to naturally lose their appeal. Regardless of your religion or faith tradition, these science-backed Ancient Secrets lead to ever-new joy. That joy is experienced right here within your nervous system, within your skin. Become a bold pioneer in consciousness, blazing the trail to your most meaningful and wildest dreams. By clearing a wide-open, unimpeded trail for easy access between your physical spine and your metaphysical Joy Source, your self-mastery begins.

Prepare yourself by committing now to becoming a practicing master of calm efficiency, boldness, fun, and fierce joy, all while maintaining your tender heart.

Introduction

Mankind's Creation and Pure Joy Creation

O nce we entered that embryonic spine and brain, we began coinciding in these two creations. The nonstop allure of distractions in mankind's creation makes it challenging to remember and stay connected to our origins from the Joy Source's creation. My intention is for this book to serve as a reminder. You come from joy. Your true nature is joy. There is a realm of joy that always awaits you, in which you are never alone. In the following story, I share my first recollection of being simultaneously steeped in the realm of joy creation while *in* mankind's creation.

Two-Year-Old in Two Creations

At the age of two, my dad and I took a memorable road trip to a small church, El Santuario de Chimayo, founded more than two hundred years ago and is a sacred pilgrimage for miracle healing. It was memorable not only because of the lush green fields of wildflowers along the two-lane country road—but also because of what happened as I sat on the church bench inside. Most memorable was the swarm of playful, joyful, celestial light beings that saturated the very air. I recall the swell of joy in my own little being, assuming everyone else there, including my dad, was having the same experience.

While the rustic interior was filled with statues of saints and holy figures, along with a huge Christ on the cross straight ahead in my sight line, it was my delightful interactions with the swarm of light beings that I most enjoyed. I felt at home.

I wanted to stay there forever. When Dad said, "Let's go," I was saddened to leave. I craved to return there until adulthood, and I did. When I was twenty-five, Dad honored my request to take me back to Chimayo. Unfortunately, it had become touristy. There were throngs of people, warning signs in the parking lot to lock your car to prevent theft, surveillance cameras, and lines. While the town had lost most of its rustic charm, I was nonetheless overwhelmed by the feeling of home, and the joy of being in powerful faith vibrations, along with the swarm of light beings. I could've stayed there all day long, but again, Dad was ready to leave before I was. Overall, I'd satisfied my two-year-old desire.

To this day, living from the joy realm and creating sanctuary within and around me has been my fierce intention wherever I live. Attaining this in mankind's loony-bin creation has been a painful, arduous struggle at times. Fortunately, in adolescence I stumbled upon, or perhaps by sheer will and desire, I discovered great masters who taught me Ancient Secrets in maintaining fierce joy.

Moving into adulthood, life conspired for me to eventually teach what I learned from the masters and to share with others. The doors to teaching opened to numerous cross sections of society. I was referred to teach at hospitals, the military, at-risk youth K–6, university, renowned resorts, conferences, festivals, and even in the media when Paramount Studios chose me to create a traditional yoga video for the mind-body series on their *Buns of Steel* fitness label.

Even though I was in demand out in the mainstream, I kept my multisensory faculties to myself because I knew it would freak out most people. I understand. Some are only comfortable with what they can know from the basic five physical senses. I honor that.

I discovered that the Ancient Secrets of the masters work for everyone. Being called to serve thousands of people in these major institutions and seeing consistent results has emboldened me to share my secret world and come out of the mystical closet.

Finally, there came a time when I felt validated by the mainstream while in a movie theater. The film *Hereafter*, a 2010 supernatural drama written and directed by Clint Eastwood and starring Matt Damon, was the closest depiction to my experience with the supernatural I'd ever seen on the big screen. I was stunned to see such a close depiction of my experience.

His character was a simple, tenderhearted blue-collar worker who sensed everything, the beauty, and the truth, which is often painful. Back then, reviewers touted it as woo-woo. I related to Matt's character so deeply that I later watched it at home so I could pause the film and cry to my heart's content. It was super awkward being in the theater, trying to refrain from what Oprah calls the "ugly cry." The deep emotional release took me by surprise. His experience of trying to fit into mankind's loony-bin creation, along with the film's sound effects and visuals, was the closest thing I'd ever seen to capturing the way I experience lightning flashes of insight, intuition, and visions. In fact, it was Oscar nominated for visual effects.

This film depicted my experience of the two creations: the eternal creation of beauty and truth within, which is primary, and mankind's repetitiously dense and temporal creation. Our original purity is buried under the conditioning from mankind's creation. Like the film's character, we're all multisensory beings, but in a culture that cultivates conformity and consumption, we favor memorizing data rather than creating. Our individuality, joy, and originality get squashed. Our intuition gets shut down.

The Ancient Secrets, when practiced, consistently reveal the purity of joy that you come from, the purity that is your true nature. While the external creation that we see through our two eyes is filled with constantly changing circumstances, our internal creation, the source of ever-renewing joy, is always available through literal insight, taking sight inward.

Since childhood, I clearly sensed the falsehoods of mankind's creation. Perhaps you did too. The vibratory rates and emotions of others' intentions, roles, status, titles, positions, and words did not always match. Deception and illusion were evident. While I didn't have the words at those preverbal stages, I knew ahead what the general outcome would be in situations, beneficial or destructive. I felt joyful anticipation from the higher vibrations and anxious foreboding from the denser vibrations being transmitted around me. These abilities to sense so much felt like a curse until I found great master teachers, guiding influences, and celestial beings to support me in trusting and living from the pure substance of life.

Finally, with great perseverance, discipline, focus, and masterful support, I have learned to enjoy balance within the two creations. During this journey, learning to live from the inside purity to the outside, my dual life as entertainer and mystic has continually opened doors for me to teach these Secrets to the mainstream and exemplify joy. The masters instructed me, "Put joy out there."

What I witnessed in all the places that I've taught and the variety of demographics that I've shared with, the layers of mankind's limiting conditioning has the same results on everyone. Not knowing and not practicing these Ancient Secrets results in what we call human nature, overwhelm, anxiety, fear, doubt, selfishness, greed, and being victimized or victimizing others.

Teaching at a university for over two decades has been particularly revealing because as I've moved forward in chronological age, each generation of students has remained within the age range of eighteen to twenty-six. While the circumstances of the world are different for every generation, the common concerns that I hear *every* semester remain the same. They express anxiety, overwhelm, stress, fear of the unknown, fear of rejection, and sometimes a dangerous desperation to belong and to receive another's approval.

Another commonality among the generations of these young adults is a buoyant curiosity for self-discovery. There's an eagerness to figure out how to responsibly contribute something meaningful to the world while having fun. Knowing the painful struggles of going through that age myself, I decided to offer a proposal for a course based on what I learned from the great master teachers I was fortunate to learn from. My university supervisor immediately gave my course the green light to teach the students the Ancient Secrets.

She was aware that these young adults need these "skills that go beyond the academic brain" and that a degree is not sufficient for attuning to the rich, individual, inner resources that we all possess. It is with great satisfaction that I witness their consistent results semester after semester as they begin to connect daily with the purity of the joy creation and the superpowers within their brain and spine.

They begin to radiate a calm glow of ease and confidence. The feelings of overwhelm diminish as they begin systematically fulfilling their dreams with calm efficiency. Many take my courses repeatedly, and their surefootedness in the world increases. They sense there's more to them than their academic brain, the skill of memorization, and blind acceptance of the status quo. With the Secrets, they realize that they sensed correctly, and they can trust the information from their Joy Source.

Over the years, students have shared their experiences of intuition, signs, synchronicities, and the supernatural. Healing tears, joy tears, deep gratitude, and goose bumps become normalized. They feel assured and comforted in knowing that these are natural gifts of life. There's a mutual respect and insightful sharing among us, which gives me great faith in their stewardess of the world.

The purity is always *right here* within us, yet the connection deepens each time the layers of conditioning are penetrated. This is the case with me and all demographics I teach and have taught, not just the university students.

In the pages ahead you will find how you, too, can easily begin now, as you are and where you are, to apply the hacks to identify who and what is in alignment with your purity of heart. You will feel the increased well-being as you begin investing energy in those directions while eliminating the distracters. Facing challenges and imbalanced circumstances will become an adventure to look forward to as a means of great self-mastery. By blazing the trail daily through external conditioning and connecting with the pure substance of life within, you will receive clarity, solutions, guidance, inspiration, and answers while *embodying* joy, calmness, and health.

Chaos, misery, and resentment result from the dangerous habit of approval-seeking.

Oh, and humor is a by-product of the Secrets. By keeping your biochemistry thoroughly saturated with flowing joy endorphins, along with your increasing awareness, you'll begin to see the absurdities in mankind's loony-bin creation. You'll gain perspective and understanding of yourself and human nature.

In 2008, I began doing stand-up comedy open mics to get myself out of a painful rut I'd been in. Studying the craft became a passion. I started getting spots in lineups and moved up. After performing as a headliner a few times, which was fun, I realized it's not a lifestyle that suits my nature. However, somewhere along the way it occurred to me that the great comedian Jerry Seinfeld, the Dalai Lama, and I had something in common. We laugh a lot, and we tend to laugh at the *pettiness and absurdities of human nature*: mankind's creation.

Then, lo and behold, I discovered that Jerry Seinfeld has been practicing the Secrets since adolescence. What I'd sensed was confirmed.

As you read ahead, I share the scientific and mystical connection between stress relief and comic relief within your body and brain. A broadened perspective, even humor and laughter, increases as you view mankind's loony-bin creation from the beauty of your inner joy creation.

Grown-Ups Have Issues

At the age of five, an experience revealed to me that grown-ups clearly have issues. There was a grandmotherly ally who lived around the corner whom my mother approved of. The neighbor qualified as my ally because she delighted in treating me to milk and freshly baked chocolate chip cookies. This was a classic win-win situation for any kid because I delighted in consuming unlimited amounts, which my mother would likely have not approved of. My mouth waters at the memory of the chewy, warm cookies with melted chips.

However, I shake my head to this day at the memory of my encounters with her equally elderly husband, who was *always* sitting on the front porch. *Every* time I visited, without fail, the old man would begin lamenting to me about his miserable life, as if I was some miniature sagely psychotherapist for him to purge his pent-up lifetime accumulation of dark demons onto. This was also my first wordless realization that grown-ups not only had issues, but repeating patterns. He repeated his same complaints every visit, like a squawking parrot stuck on its perch. I recall his unkempt gray hair, scruffy and looking like the Brillo pads that were used back then for scrubbing dish pans.

His pitiful expression created a permanent furrowed brow. His forehead wrinkles were deep enough to hold a dime, like the treads on new car tires. He whined and whined to me that he didn't do what he wanted with his life because his wife, my generous cookie source, wouldn't let him. He "would have, could have . . . if it wasn't for her." Perhaps he desperately hoped someone, even me a virtual toddler, would turn against his wife and stick up for him.

His desperate attempts to vilify her fell on deaf ears. I didn't judge him; I simply observed as children do and noted that his attitude matched his contorted-looking facial expression. From my little-girl view, I felt a blend of pity and puzzlement about how a grown-up arrived at this state of being.

It was startling to realize that I couldn't count on even the oldest of the old grown-ups in my world to be examples of emotional stability, nor fun! With my feet aimed toward the screen door, I would nod speechlessly and try to politely flee into the house for my intended purpose. I felt relief and anticipation as I finally made it to a seat at the dining table, my feet dangling from the grown-up chair, ready to be served. Talk about taking the bitter with the sweet. His story has been a cautionary tale ever since.

I didn't ask, but wordless questions rumbled in my head. He emanated a vibration, a palpable unpleasant frequency. How could another person, his wife in this case, stop this able-bodied grown man from doing what he wants? Why didn't he stand up, get up, and do what he wanted to do with his life? He could stand. He could walk. He could talk. Why was he dumping this on me, burdening me? Why was he giving me unspoken authority to help him?

It was difficult to wrap my little-girl brain around these adult dynamics, yet I distinctly made a choice in that moment that I would *not* be like him. If I can help it, nobody and nothing is going to stop me from enjoying my life when I grow up. While I didn't have the words to identify what I observed then, there were attitudes expressed by the grown-ups that I silently vowed to *never* model.

Revisiting these childhood memories, I eventually found the words *blame* and *regret*. These were the two main culprits that resulted in the misery I witnessed in the old man on the porch. Since then, I have struggled to discover my own individual voice, to become the final authority of my life and boldly express it. I vehemently decided in that moment that I will take full responsibility for my life!

From then on, I distinctly recall tilting my head a lot, filled with silent questions, looking up at the adults in my world, observing that oftentimes what they said and did simply did not make sense; some actually looked quite crazy, flying off the handle. In my little-girl mind, I realized I would have to bide my time until adulthood when I would be free to choose what made sense for me. While under the necessary care of adults, like all children, I received the common spoken and unspoken message that external authorities always know what's best. Because of this conditioning, as an adult I frequently lost myself by sacrificing my internal authority, resulting in chaos, pain, and even resentment, flat-out drained. I occasionally became like the whiney old man.

Phew, thanks to the lesson learned from the example of the old man on the porch, I passionately searched for what suits my nature and brings me joy. This exploration has led me to discover the Ancient Secrets that attune us to our inner authority. These result in continuity of peace, *embodying* calm efficiency, fun, and a tender heart, free, free, free of blame and regret.

By attuning to my inner authority, I've come to greatly value mastering the calmness that creates the inner atmosphere conducive to *listening* to the beautiful faculty of the soul: intuition. I listen to what my heart and soul are calling me to do while observing and steering clear of the joy robbers of limiting attitudes, my own and those projected onto me from family, friends, society, business associates, media, and the culture.

The Secrets can be mixed and matched, like a menu of treats, depending on the current soulful needs of your inner atmosphere and the conditions coming at you from your outer atmosphere. The Secrets lead you to the countless gifts of life and safety. Once you have a history of success under your belt, you will develop complete trust in your benevolent intuition.

Next, I'll share with you the exciting science of your baby spine and brain, your body's first system and first organ, where your source of joy flows in and resides. By regularly accessing and maintaining your joy connection, you begin your practicing master adventure.

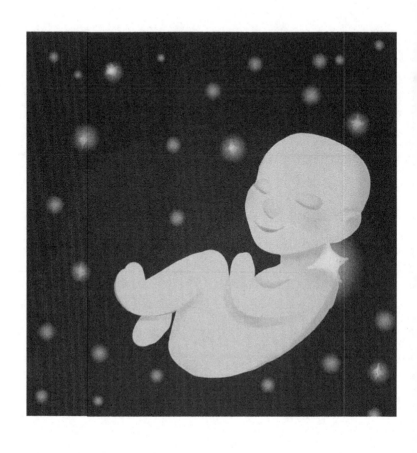

CHAPTER 1

Your Joy Source

Hidden Power in Your Brain and Spine

Mystically, your spine and brain are God's terrain, where the pure substance of life first began expressing into your body. Literally, the spine and brain are at the very core of your being. This may be the reason for the saying, "Man cannot live by bread alone." As morbid as it sounds, no amount of bread stuffed into a corpse will enliven that flesh.

The Secrets reveal the primary source of our embodied energy, making the mystical practical. This practicality allows for surefooted maneuvering in mankind's creation. To transmute this mystical power from your Joy Source into material practicality, we will first delve into the mechanics of your body and how to work with the parts to keep your body vehicle running at optimum levels. This is key to finding spiritual solutions to any issue and your source of impervious fierce joy.

Just as a car has mechanical parts, there are primary energy systems that you were born with. Warning! While we'd rather not think about *exactly* what our parents were doing, be grateful they did it. You get to be here! When the sperm and ovum met and you were conceived, your brain and spine began forming where the top of the neck meets the skull. This physical point of conception is prevertebral. Respectively, your embryonic brain and spinal nerves were the first organ and system to develop from this point. The electromagnetic forces of life, infinite Joy Source, flowed into your brain and spine. While babies are often referred to as a bundle of joy, they are also a literal bundle of nerves, here to have as much fun as possible while practicing self-mastery.

This is where you manage your power, within these systems. You are in charge of cleansing and calming your nerves. You can live from joy by returning to the innocence originating from your baby spine and brain. With the Secrets, we become aware of the murky densities that have accumulated on the nerves and energy centers. Then we can systematically release the murk to reveal our pure, impervious joy.

With some basic knowledge of the machinations of our body vehicle, we will begin to explore what it takes to keep it running smoothly. By distinguishing the various results of habits, we can consciously choose the quality of experience we aim for and our ideal way of being in the world.

Baby Spine Care – Discernment

Your baby spine is the *physical* manifestation of the *metaphysical* spinal energy channel connected to your

Joy Source, the source your soul comes from. This chapter will help you understand and manage the quality of what you are broadcasting to the world from your channel while becoming aware of what you are receiving from outside sources. With the Secrets, you will gain clarity for distinguishing the ego's defensive reactions, the emotion's potential for rash impulsiveness, and the soul's desire for peaceful, flowing, loving choices. This knowledge equips you to boldly face whatever's in front of you, and by applying the Secrets daily, you'll begin creating a cumulative effect of ever greater good.

The benefits of joy and self-mastery will increase over time, becoming your regular way of being in the world. You will begin moving from chaos-generating distractions to calm efficiency. Pleasures and even challenges become fun as you strengthen and deepen your connection to the source of your joy power. Rather than allowing blame and regret to fuel bitterness, you will find that fiercely protecting your peace will nurture an inner atmosphere for your tender heart to flourish in joy. Joy is your protection!

Initially, you may feel reluctant concern about your ability to relinquish unhealthy habits. Many habits are used as a coping mechanism or to fill a void. So, continue to forge ahead with sincere attempts at mastering the Ancient Secrets. Over time, as happened with me and others, the calmness, well-being, and flow that take over will make the appeal of unhealthy habits pale by comparison. And, over time, you will come to know that the company of joy found within cannot be topped by any fleeting pleasures of the temporal, external creation. This skill of discerning the quality of habits puts you on the road to a freeing perspective, free of the need for others' approval.

Cultures and Values – Two Different Things

There's the phrase: "Dark night of the soul." I experienced what I call the dark of the soul for seven *years*. I'm not competing to be the biggest victim; we all have our challenges. Nobody escapes being victimized in one way or another on planet Earth. The depth of loneliness during this time was deep and intensified over the holidays due to cultural habits and traditions I was taught to give meaning to. So, in this sense, the loneliness was a result of societal conditioning, which I, as an adult with choice, could perpetuate or change. With the fierce joy resulting from the Secrets, I chose to change.

When you, the baby, arrived in the world, the conditioning of traditions and beliefs by others was written on the slate of your being and encoded in your brain and nerves. You can return to your purity of being daily by cleaning the slate with the Secrets.

Over the years, since childhood, I was keenly aware that family members, say an average of four out of fifteen, at gatherings would cause conflict, expressing sarcasm; one even had a knack for regularly raging and name-calling. As a child and into adulthood, I was always puzzled as to why the many would cower to these few. You know how dogs turn their heads sideways when something doesn't make sense? That's exactly how I felt at family gatherings. While there'd be some genuine, thoughtful conversations, lots of laughter, and we always sang together, the spoilsports could be counted on to burst bubbles, hurt feelings, insult, intimidate . . . Everyone would walk on eggshells around these joy robbers. I see now that these social dynamics were a microcosm of the world at large—common.

From what I understand, most, if not every family, has dysfunction, but it never made sense to me that just because I was biologically related to someone that I was obligated to expose myself to abusive behavior. Because I seemed to be the only one in my family who was willing to see what I saw happening, question it, and not put my head in the sand, I eventually declared that I would no longer attend any function where predictably abusive people would attend. I chose to see who I wanted to see before or after these gatherings. I was no longer attached to the date of a holiday on the calendar. I value enjoying every day of life more than following limiting cultural conditioning.

This caused a ripple through the tribe. "How could you break the cultural traditions? Blood is thicker than water. . . ." So, I created my own ways of celebrating. One Christmas night, I enjoyed reading the shaman, don Miguel Ruiz's book, *The Mastery of Love*, front to back, with a picture of Jesus on a chair next to me. Another year, two friends were stuck alone, very ill, and I drove three hours to bring each one a care package, wiped their fevered brows, and just sat with them. Admittedly, I did cry and grieve during that period, yet that was far better than subjecting myself to the draining joy robbers. During these emotionally challenging times I learned to clearly distinguish whose values matched mine, biologically related or not. I've grown accustomed to delighting in and unofficially adopting and being adopted by cool people who are kind, civil, supportive, and respectful—qualities I value. Aligned values mean more to me than tradition.

I'm so grateful for those lonely years. I came out on the other side of that experience thoroughly enjoying the best company of all, the impervious joy that is not contingent on outer circumstances. The healing tears of grief cleansed away the shattered illusions of limited conditioning and revealed the Joy Source within me. I'm telling you, life is freaky fun when you enjoy being you!

Confidence and Anxiety – The Struggle

When I began practicing meditation at age thirteen, I didn't dare speak of it to my peers, as I knew that I'd be bullied. Back then, it was nowhere near as mainstream as it is now. People who meditated were commonly called derogatory names. Combining that with adolescent peer pressure would have been a setup for sheer cruelty.

As I practiced the Secrets in silence, I felt my inner being change. I sensed the calm glow of serenity increasing within me and radiating around me. I recall another teenager in the neighborhood looking at me side-eyed, curiously asking me, "What are you doing? You seem different." I didn't dare disclose the Secrets, as he quickly mocked others over the slightest little thing. I feigned ignorance, like I had no idea what he was talking about, as I did for another decade. That was until neuroscientists and quantum physicists began to make the validity of the mystical Secrets common knowledge.

I understand what it takes to get over the fear of ridicule and shaming from others, being treated as an outcast. Even later in adulthood, a "friend" from junior high called me weird, even though I had been chosen to create an internationally distributed yoga video for my "weirdness." My conditioned approval-seeking personality tolerated digs from this so-called friend for a few more years.

Hearing others talk of having friends since childhood was an ego trap for me. I realized that I rationalized her abusiveness simply because we had shared history. Culture praises friendship longevity, like it's something to brag about, but the disparity in our values was a drain on my joy. Her last put-down of my accomplishments was the final nail in the coffin. I blessed and released her in my mind and blocked her on my phone and social media. I've since changed my definition of friendship. Having a long history together is not enough to qualify for true friendship.

Looking at my confidence on stage, you wouldn't know I struggled with low self-esteem. Societal and cultural conditioning taught me that expressing joy for my accomplishments wasn't safe or acceptable. I would do what I wanted to do, yet I went through years of feeling anxiety-ridden. While I have been focused and disciplined in my efforts to express my passions, it's been a painful ride accepting that even supposed family and friends sometimes felt and acted with bitter jealousy. Some have been downright dangerous and sabotaging.

Masters warned me of this painful, ugly truth about human nature and offered this advice:

Disregard. Don't bother reprimanding those who express jealousy, just keep moving in your own direction.

Through much soul-searching and support groups, I eventually realized that there were two forces in this world: those capable of being supportive and those who would mock my efforts and diminish every accomplishment. Somehow, I still managed to move forward with sweaty palms until I developed an unshakable connection to joy. With this solid connection, I learned to celebrate and own my gifts, expressing that joy regardless of others' opinions. I now easily accept that if someone is uncomfortable with my living fully, it's best not to be around them. Parting is best for both of us.

After a while, I began building in secret to fulfill my dreams and move forward unhampered. I wouldn't let anyone know what I was doing. That was between me and my Joy Source. The response to my accomplishments was celebrated with joy by those who were secure with themselves. Apparently, those who had a competitive eye on me were angry that I did not tell them what I was doing or expressed surprise that I had moved forward so quickly.

That was their perception, but the truth was they were unaware that I put daily effort into inquiring and listening to my Joy Source. I then followed through with a combination of exploration, research, study, planning, rehearsing, and taking responsible risks. Building in secret was necessary because I habitually let myself be distracted by tiresome negative forces. Now, silently taking action toward dreams feels right and natural. Everyone is responsible for discovering their soul contribution to the world, and it really is nobody else's business. Letting that Joy Source build and saturate your every effort is precious and worth putting boundaries around to satisfy the completion of meaningful goals. I do what I do because I enjoy it, and that is enough. If others find value and benefit from my service, that is my intention, but if they don't, they can go elsewhere. Nothing's lost because I still enjoy what I'm doing. Either way, when you have this attitude, you win.

What helped me shift from low self-esteem to confidence was deliberately training myself to focus on those who are kind and supportive. Those who are derogatory are out!

Joy robbers get no access to my personal world. I now easily celebrate my own gifts with every daily step I take. I welcome those who nurture my spirit. In turn, I am ridiculously delighted when I see others fully expressing their gifts. They inspire me! I truly love seeing people thrive in peace, health, and joy.

Are there super kind, supportive people in your world that you may be overlooking? I highly recommend that you train yourself to focus on investing your time and energy in them while weeding out the draining joy robbers. Seek out, value, and express appreciation to those rare people who are consistently respectful, those who genuinely wish you well, and those who have your best interest at heart. Rather than blindly accepting my suggestions, make these relationship changes at your own pace, and ideally, after connecting in calmness to Joy Source for clarity and understanding. You'll see the quality of your life dramatically improve.

You can continually improve the quality of your life by checking daily the quality of your interactions with others. Balanced social connections lead to peaceful, flowing, loving experiences. The Ancient Secrets will help you apprehend truth and discern what is untruth, making the way clear for maintaining the connection to Joy Source. This will make the difference between sinking into the quicksands of the world and flourishing forward on solid ground.

Invalidators

In my experience, those who try to get you to doubt yourself have something to hide: insecurity, fear, nefarious agendas, and, sometimes, even illegal behaviors. Invalidation is an epidemic in mankind's loony-bin creation. Invalidation is a draining transmitted Bid for Energy (BFE), resulting in diminished joy. Fortunately, this form of abuse is coming to the awareness of the masses with trending social media about the prevalence of gas lighting. Gas lighting, based on the classic film *Gaslight*, is another term for invalidation. The invalidating behaviors are meant to put self-doubt in a person's mind for selfish gain. It's one of the most heinous things people do to each other, manipulating a person to doubt their God-given awareness, their personal truth, their intuition. It's human nature to be in another's business, to be snoopy, and to find any reason to feel superior to one another. Invalidation—trying to get someone to doubt themselves is one way to establish false authority over another.

Sharing your beautiful experiences, visions, and dreams revealed to you from the purity of your Joy Source is not meant for the public and its potential joy robbers. Your visions come to you for you to fulfill. Let your joy power fuel your actions. When you build in secret, joy robbers won't know what to attack or invalidate.

Even when you are clear about what you sense, and your experience is undeniable, there are those who will invalidate, play devil's advocate, or plant seeds of doubt. Some invalidation not only comes from individuals, "friends," family members, or spouses, but also from groups and organizations. One national organization run by corrupt, greedy individuals tried to shut me down when I went to human resources to complain about a hostile supervisor. I discovered the HR staff was equally corrupt. I complained about a rat, but it came out in an investigative report on the news that there was an entire nest of corrupt rats. It was exhausting, but I and many others were validated by the news report and the lawsuits won against them.

Another extreme case of tribal invalidation happened when I moved into a beautiful, dreamy apartment. One noisy neighbor in the building was tyrannically inconsiderate and acted entitled with a level of sociopathic hostility and violent tendencies. During my first week, I took a risk and gently knocked at the noisy neighbor's door at 1:00 a.m. to request quiet. Because of the neighbor's flagrant selfishness, I figured receiving an apology would be highly unlikely but hoped for the best. Unfortunately, my logic was right. She sneered and snapped. I quietly retreated, resigned to the fact that there was a selfish, inconsiderate loony in the building. Cars came and went, men came and went, every night between 11:00 p.m. and 3:00 a.m., her "clients" stomping up and down stairs, the building door opening and closing. She escalated her audacious, retaliatory domination of the building.

All tenants were too intimidated to speak up about her flagrantly running a prostitution ring. Instead, they were cowardly complaining to the mail lady, but took no action. The next three tenants who shared a common wall with the prostitute all moved out within months. I turned inward for direction from my fierce Joy Source, receiving clear and useful ideas for action and intuitive guidance for when it was time for nonaction. After consecutive weeks of sleep deprivation, my intuition led me to design and print official-looking signs with noise ordinance laws, requesting consideration for neighbors who may be sleeping. In the dark morning light, I then took the authority to post the signs at the entrance and exit doors of the building. It worked. She began sneaking clients in more quietly. This was a vast improvement.

The wisdom that comes from intuition provides solutions from beyond the usual looping thinking mind. It provides alternatives from your gut—calm, fierce knowing. Violators, habitual joy robbers, do not get the usual emotional reaction they're used to when you act with such conscious responses. It's quite an adventure to go beyond the cogitating mind and begin following the intuition from your pure Joy Source.

In these situations, I don't get even; I get odd. Intuition is always fresh and odd, compared to the predictable ideas of the ruminating mind. The guidance always provides the best of self-care tactics while being harmless to others. Joy robbers will always be bitter when their thievery is thwarted, but that's their responsibility.

Gradually the bitter prostitute toned down, began doing outcall, and finally moved out. The truth was eventually revealed, as it always is. The mail lady befriended me and shared that a former tenant incessantly complained about the disruptive noise created by the prostitute. It was going on long before I moved in, but others tolerated the heinously selfish, entitled behavior. After she moved out, other tenants felt free and began referring to her unit as the "former hooker hotel." The ruckus she caused and the fear and intimidation tactics she used are common strategies from those who try to deflect others from seeing the ugly, painful emptiness and shameful truth they feel about themselves. They've lost connection to their Joy Source.

To clarify, I do not condemn her chosen line of service in the world. I was simply committed to maintaining a peaceful, harmonious environment for myself, a sanctuary. The experience of being in the realm of angels and light beings in that little chapel at the age of two with my dad set the standard for me. They let me know that they are with me every step of the way, even and especially in this challenging situation.

Every invalidator in my life played a role that helped me increase my conviction to trust my intuitive knowing and firmly establish myself in unshakable fierce joy.

Graduations in Consciousness

It takes ferocity to face and stand in truth, to maintain connection to your Joy Source in mankind's loony-bin creation. The prostitute vied to rule a small building on a corner, on this mud ball of earth floating in a vast universe. That's a small temporal trinket compared to the beautiful, lasting treasure of infinite joy within your being. Her fear and intimidation tactics were understandable because she used her home to conduct business, and anybody who complained was a threat to her "job security." Meanwhile, being more determined than ever, I vied only to be master of myself, nobody else, and continue to dwell in the purity of infinitely fierce joy.

No matter my street address, my constant habitat is within me, within my skin. I am in charge of the quality of my inner atmosphere, my constant place of dwelling. Externally, I followed reasoning and explored moving, but that wasn't practical for me at the time. When I find myself thwarted from leaving a situation, I know there's a valuable lesson for me to face and learn. This inspires me to use the Secrets to connect with joy and listen for my steps to freedom.

In this particular situation, I gave myself respites from the menacing neighbor by booking monthly comedy gigs out of town, which is always fun. Fortuitously, lots of other business during this period required travel, making my schedule unpredictable. The obsessive neighbor, with her unusual interest in me, was disrupted in her ability to track me.

When joy robbers start developing a pattern with you, alter your routine. Give yourself a change of scenery to create distance from their chaos; restore your calmness. Every boundary violation signals that it's time for a self-care upgrade, and every self-care upgrade is cause for celebration. It symbolizes that yet another beautiful lesson has been more deeply locked in, reinforcing your fierce joy.

Leaving no stone unturned, working with what I had within my power, I used this challenging time as an opportunity to expand the beauty of my Soul Wall, my inner fortress of joy. I continued deepening the practice of the Secrets while consciously embodying and affirming, "I am dwelling in beauty, peace, and goodness." I energetically expanded my Soul Wall with the Secrets to block the prostitute's unseen—but felt—projected bids for toxic energy connection.

Her demonic desire for an emotional reaction was silently rejected as sod under my feet. I sensed any emotional reaction toward this tortured soul would have given her a distraction from her desperate feelings of joy deficiency. By *Soul Wall*, I am referring to the purity that comes from Joy Source. By expanding your joy capacity, you are expanding your Soul Wall of protection. During this experience, I could feel all old fear patterns gradually crumbling away while I continually transformed every BFE from the prostitute into an unshakable connection to calmness, tenderness, and fierce joy.

This was the experience I cultivated in my inner atmosphere and eventually experienced in the literal walls of the building. I took responsibility for my frequency. Frequencies are personal vibrations created by the emotions we frequently cultivate. Beauty, peace, and goodness frequencies expanded from my Soul Wall into the very walls of the building.

However, the changes in the building were secondary; the boldness and self-mastery I attained are the primary and permanent treasures that I sought and succeeded in attaining through this experience. This is what I consider winning. She could keep her bitterness and temporarily win the rule of a building. I maintained the sovereignty of myself, embodying fierce joy, tenderness, and even generosity of spirit.

I seized the opportunity to extend a kindness to the malicious tenant the week she was moving out by alerting her that she left her car parked in a way that would result in a ticket. While I inwardly sensed that I had mastered myself in this situation, extending kindness that day confirmed outwardly that I officially graduated from the lesson. She moved the car without a thank-you, but that didn't matter. I inwardly celebrated while simultaneously reaffirming, "I am dwelling in beauty, peace, and goodness."

I truly am grateful that I got to express that goodness. I remained free of her baits of bitterness and protected my soul with fierce joy. Yippee! All while maintaining tenderness within. Joy is my true habitat, no matter where I am on the planet. You don't obtain a degree in consciousness from these graduations, but the increased mastery simultaneously increases your capacity for fun, clearing the way for life's next batch of countless gifts to flow to you ever more abundantly.

The transitions from infancy to adolescence to becoming a young adult are very marked in terms of development. Once adulthood is established, tracking significant transitions needs to be increasingly conscious and ideally prepared for. Otherwise, your evolutionary steps can be overlooked and blurred with habitual behaviors and become ruts. Being in this loony-bin world is challenging, and the Ancient Secrets prepare you to boldly face anything. These experiences offer opportunities to graduate to new levels of mastery. Acknowledge every small win daily. Honor and celebrate every graduation in consciousness.

At each level of mastery, you can expect an increased flow of life's countless gifts. It's a natural outcome. I expect it. You, too, can fortify and expand the beauty of your Soul Wall by setting forth actions into motion directly from your Joy Source. Consider your ever-expanding Soul Wall as the container of all your goodness, including calmness, fun, and tenderness. Life presents opportunities daily, disguised as challenges to increase the radiance of your Soul Wall.

Who Defines You

By seeking validation from others, you are broadcasting a bid for an external connection and external approval. Recognition for gifts, talents, and accomplishments feels good, but seeking and expecting validation is risky. There is no shortage of people who would gladly manipulate you with your bid in seeking their approval. They span the spectrum from online and global swindlers to immediate biological relatives. Some will view you as a resource to utilize for attention, time, and money or to rob you of your joy.

It requires so much discipline and focus to discover and reveal the callings from your heart and soul that it is impossible for others, who don't even know themselves, to know or understand the depths of your heart's callings.

Maintaining your integrity is the only validation you need. Integrity implies wholeness and the integration of your values with your actions. Only in business do we really need external validation (in the form of compensation to pay bills). Let yourself be defined from the purity of Joy Source. Feel genuine appreciation for your own efforts while allowing joy to touch all you do. If others choose to genuinely celebrate and honor you, that is a gift to be appreciated; these are valued supporters, yet nobody's opinion is required for you to know your Joy Source. Know thyself. This is your responsibility.

Identifying Joy Robbers and Joy Traps

This is where some of the fun focus comes into play. After developing keen awareness and clear intuition from the Secrets, you will begin sensing the strange malevolent intentions of others in advance. Something will feel off. It's like sensing a predictable movie plot, where you know the inevitable painful outcome of the characters' interactions. The only difference is that in your life, you will thwart the villains with your fun, amazing, intuitive solutions. These solutions protect and guide you to your personal life package of abundance provided by your Joy Source. You'll master slipping out of the joy robbers' grip and avoiding the power-tripping traps altogether. While nobody in this loony-bin world of mankind's creation goes without being victimized at some point, the Secrets will free you from being stuck in the victim role.

Here at earth school, we unwittingly fall into traps repeatedly until we catch on. The best way to avoid the traps is by remembering and knowing that your true identity is joy. Joy is the protective attribute of your soul. When we forget who we are, we get ourselves into all kinds of pickles.

Below, I've listed seven of the most common traps that I've witnessed and experienced:

1. Tug o' War

You might recall playing the childhood game of two or more holding opposite ends of a rope. The idea was to tug forcefully enough to tug the rope out of the hands of the "opponents." Metaphorically, adults act out a similar dynamic of trying to gain power over the "rope" of title, credit for an idea, or inheritance. The list goes on and on. From my perspective, nothing is worth power-struggling over that will diminish my health or joy connection. To remain free of this trap of pettiness, I drop the rope, all resistance, and walk away into broader horizons. In the childhood game, if you drop the rope in the middle of the tugging match, the "opponent" wins the rope but lands on their arse. Continue moving in your own direction to ever broader, more fun, abundant horizons with your tender heart intact.

2. Carrot Danglers

A major vulnerability to traps is caused by approval-seeking. Seeking external validation is a state of wanting, of lack, forgetting that your true, abundant identity and source is pure joy. Approval seekers are prey to carrot danglers who make the carrot, that approval seekers desperately want, forever inaccessible. This trap is a means of control and a frustrating drain on precious joy. The term *carrot dangler* originates from farmers rigging a carrot to dangle in front of a mule's face. As the mule unwittingly chased the unreachable carrot, it inadvertently plowed the field for the farmer's gain. I also refer to carrot danglers as withholders. Once I identify this trap, I immediately move on and want nothing from these time-wasting scenarios.

3. False Sense of Guilt

If you've been conditioned to overgive with a false sense of obligation to others, you will become prey to predatory joy robbers. They will accuse you of being selfish. This is done by manipulating and inducing feelings of guilt in order to continue taking. They'll take until you've lost all sense of self and more. Continually giving to and sharing with greedy, unappreciative people will leak and eventually drain the joy out of you. When you cut off the joy robbers and begin to take care of yourself, it will feel unnatural at first. Continue to white-knuckle your way through to Joy Source until you become the very embodiment of fierce joy.

And to reiterate the point, joy is the protective attribute of your soul. Stay closely connected to your Joy Source. Those who are deceitful, betraying others, severely lack their connection to joy. They might experience fleeting glee by acquiring at another's expense, but that will never be as satisfying as being in the state of pure joy.

4. Bubble Busters

Another trap is set by bubble busters who will diminish your joy and deflate you like a balloon to keep you under their thumb. One minute, you're enthusiastically sharing about something you're looking forward to, and the bubble buster says something like, "Oh, that's no big deal," or perhaps apathetically changes the subject altogether. In this case, your joy is best kept to yourself and shared only with sincerely supportive people. Most importantly, celebrate yourself, every small win, every day. Eventually you will develop impervious fierce joy.

There are all kinds of bait to beware of. Bait is used to manipulate a reaction (an unhealthy BFE). If you fly off the handle with an emotional reaction, that means that you took the bait, hook, line, and sinker. This is exactly what joy robbers are after. Other bubble-busting traps are put-downs and negatively comparing you to others. *You* have something the joy robber wants: an emotional reaction.

5. Defensiveness

Becoming self-aware of defensiveness is one of my favorites. I really do get excited when I identify this one and free myself of defensiveness by remembering my true identity: joy. Defensiveness is a clear predecessor to overreacting, overexplaining, and a complete waste of energy, especially when trying to prove a point to someone with different values, who wants to convince you that you're inferior in some way, or who has no genuine interest in understanding you. Each time you catch inner defensiveness, you will more immediately cut the bait and remain free. Take defensiveness as a good reminder to remember your true joy identity.

6. Expectations

Expecting from others who don't follow through leads to draining frustration. The fact is that once you're an adult, you don't owe anyone anything. Nobody owes you anything. It's unrealistic to have expectations of others. Anything given or received is ideally given freely, with joy, and acknowledged with appreciation. Yet, that cannot be expected.

Even if agreements have been made, we can only hope the parties involved have enough integrity and a strong, conscientious desire to be good on their word. We don't have to go far back into history to see that in mankind's loony-bin creation, once some people get what they want, they will breach contracts, treaties, and promises and are not good on their word. The best we can do is have a combination of documentation, backup plans, and, most ideally, a strong connection to our intuition, the faculty of our soul.

7. Jealousy

The jealousy trap is a gnarly one yet undeniably part of dense human nature. Jealousy is not of your pure joy nature. Being recognized and appreciated for an accomplishment feels momentarily good, but when you are anchored in continuity of joy, neither praise nor blame has much effect on you. Jealousy stems from an irrational belief that if I discredit or steal, sabotage or diminish someone else's good, then I will have more. Another facet of this toxic emotion is the irrational belief that if I cut someone down, I will somehow level them or become bigger than them. In reality, the result is that this person is acting petty and looking small.

Comparison and jealousy cramps joy. A jealousy cure is to use the Secrets to clear the murk to reveal and know your own beautiful Joy Source, which is not to be found outside of you. When you witness someone being, doing, or having something you'd like, stretch yourself by expressing admiration, appreciation, or honoring that person. Keep going until it feels natural for you to joyfully celebrate others.

It's fun to vicariously enjoy others' experiences and even more fun to discover, reveal, and express from your Joy Source. It goes against the laws of the Ancient Secrets to even consider living through another's Joy Source. It's impossible to do so. Attempting to do so will completely disrupt the peaceful, loving flow of life's countless gifts. No one else has your fingerprint. Your Joy Source comes complete with your own individual and original gifts to enjoy and share with the world. Do your best. Free yourself from attachment to outcome. With practice you will eventually gather a history of success with the Secrets and develop trust in what your Joy Source leads you to do.

A Baseline of Calmness

Being in your natural state of calmness and joy becomes normalized by remaining steeped in the Secrets and deeply connected to Joy Source. With calmness as your baseline, you will immediately sense when there is a disruptive ripple from an internal or external joy robber. With your fortified Soul Wall of light and awareness, the joy robber's BFE will bounce right off, keeping your channel open and receptive to the abundant flow of life's countless gifts.

You will be dancing with gratitude, a-bun-dance! You will be the embodiment of fierce joy!

Don't Be a Doormat

Remember, we don't want to be like the old man on the porch, stuck in a lifetime of the victim role, expressing nothing but blame and regret. His complaining was clearly an ingrained habit, perhaps embedded after years, maybe decades of repetition. I heard his lament every single time his wife invited me over for fresh cookies. This was evident to a five-year-old. I'm glad I caught that way back then. Even though I went in and out of the trance of approval-seeking conditioning, I repeatedly shattered those illusions with the Secrets and faced reality.

I was fortunate to have the help of my intuition and the guidance of great master teachers. Just as the pattern of approval-seeking was established over time, it takes time to form new habits and modify relationship boundaries.

Empty, antagonistic people feed off the emotional reactions of others to feel alive. During interactions where someone is making a toxic BFE, baiting you for an emotional reaction, it is human nature to slip and lose your cool on occasion.

When this happens, give yourself grace and forgiveness. The seeds of doubt that others plant create clouds of confusion. Penetrate to your Joy Source to inquire about the cause of uneasy gut feelings until you clear the clouds. Use the Secrets to return to your baseline of calmness. When you're calm, you don't make mistakes.

Listen for your answers, clear the clouds, the illusions. Joy Source always provides the next action or nonaction to take with a simple step. Understanding is found in the clarity of your unclouded purity. When others are used to you falling into their traps and sense your beautiful Soul Wall expanding, they will usually escalate tactics to keep a draining connection to your Joy Source, taxing your nerves.

When this happens, you can hunker down even deeper with the Secrets, fortifying the beauty of your Soul Wall, listening, and following the fierce, calm knowing of your intuition. In some cases, you can radiate and transmit this without saying a word. Other times your intuition may call for you to step up with some assertive action, to develop a stronger commitment to your joy connection, to develop a proverbial backbone, a spine of steel. In such situations you may be required to express what I call *reverse boldness*.

When a joy robber is bold enough to violate or victimize you, it is appropriate to face the violation boldly and set bold boundaries. Habitual approval-seekers feel unwarranted guilt for standing up for themselves. To put this response into proper perspective, consider how joy robbers boldly violate others without guilt or remorse.

Being compliant to violators dims your light by allowing your joy to be siphoned. Be determined to become free of them or you risk being bitterly stuck in a victim role. While there are predictable patterns of dense human nature, every challenging situation varies, and every day there are variables to learn from. Developing keen listening to intuition every step of the way is necessary. There's a big difference between being kind and being a doormat. Contrary to the delusive, dogmatic conditioning that people-pleasing equates with being spiritual, setting fierce boundaries from the purity of your Joy Source actually reveals your inner light automatically.

Learn the beautiful lessons and throw out the doormat!

Managing Bids for Energy

As children, we naturally broadcast BFEs to our parents to receive love, attention, and care. We are dependent and vulnerable. Infants send out BFEs nonlinguistically, without words, with gibberish sounds or a wailing cry, and physical gestures. As parents become attuned to their child's nonlinguistic BFEs, they know what the bid is about. An unseen connection develops. As adults, we are now responsible for our choices in managing our exchange of BFEs with others. Ideally, we make a BFE daily with our steady, reliable Joy Source *first* in all things. This assists in discerning the value of external bids with others.

Examples of Silent Bids for Energy

These are the thoughts, energies, intentions, and projections we send to or about others through nonlinguistic communication. When we send out a thought, it does not stay inside our brain. It transmits. Because mankind is incessantly thinking—sometimes kindly, sometimes compulsively, obsessively, and unconsciously—applying the Secrets is necessary. A daily settling of accounts and cleansing and calming the nerves within your baby spine will clear your inner atmosphere for free-flowing, abundant joy.

Discerning External Bids for Energy

1. Every call, email, snail mail, text, voicemail, or doorbell ring you receive is a BFE. Pause to consider, "What does this person want or need from me?" Before responding, inquire with yourself, "What is the best way that I should respond, or if I should respond at all, in order to maintain my focus and express respect for my precious life energy?"

2. For those personalities who tend to create chaos and crazy-making, it is always best to respond via written word, with no mention of emotions, only formal and brief one- or two-sentence responses with facts.

Those with a chaos addiction provoke and feed off emotional reactions. It's case by case, and there may be some personal learning involved, yet eventually you will want to minimize or completely cut off these types of draining distractions. This will maintain your energy for fun focus and your tender heart to flourish.

3. When others become overly familiar and begin taking you for granted and wasting your time, it's best to become very formal with them. This is why the cliché, "Familiarity breeds contempt," is true. It's just human nature; it is very common for people to treat those closest in their sphere poorly. Formality, brevity, politeness, and a professional tone help to set or reset a tone of respect. If the violators continue to act poorly, at least you are respecting yourself.

4. Written, formal emails are advisable in any type of business transaction and can be organized more easily than a text thread. When someone makes a bid for your energy in business, it's efficient to request a written proposal of the idea they are asking you to invest in. This is extremely useful for those who are not good at following through on their word or perhaps lack integrity. It's difficult to argue with the facts in written documentation, yet some loony joy robbers will try it.

With written proposals, you can take the time to pause and consider if it's a good use of your energy or a distraction from your vision. A proposal allows for fun focus in negotiations and clarification before you seal the deal with a signature. Unfortunately, sometimes people finagle and scheme even with documentation. Follow your gut. Listen to your Joy Source every step of the way.

5. Chronically late people are robbers. Allowing someone to rob your time will inevitably lead to feeling resentful. This toxic emotion will then impinge on your joy and can lead to illness. Resentment will sour your tender heart. To protect my joy from time-robbers, I plan to meet at a place *I will enjoy with or without them*. My personal waiting limit is fifteen minutes maximum, sometimes less, especially if there's no courtesy call. I will go ahead without them, order, and enjoy my meal, or at a movie, go in, get my popcorn, and secure a good seat. This turns the tables. Two time-robbers that I did this with got angry but couldn't justify their reaction because I had honored my word. After taking note of their continuing disrespectful behavior, I respected myself enough to cut them out of my life.

BID FOR ENERGY GUIDE

Three Types of BFEs:

1. **With your Joy Source.** The Secrets are expressions of your BFE with Joy Source. This type of bid is your personal connection to the very substance of life that sustains your body. This connection feels safe, comforting, replenishing, providing benevolent guidance and ever-new joy. It is as near as your breath.

2. **Transmitted from others.** These are bids sent to you from others. You can accept or reject a BFE. Some qualities of a *joyful BFE* are appreciation, mutual respect, generosity, compassion, kindness, sincerity, loyalty, and playfulness. To the contrary, some qualities of a *joy-robbing BFE* involve tactics such as antagonism, violence, intimidation, discrediting, diminishing, discounting, invalidating, and deception. If you've accepted a BFE that you realize is an imbalanced situation, leaving you feeling drained, confused, and anxious or violated in any way, this will not only leak your joy, but tax your nerves and health.

If the person transmitting the BFE does not want to come into balance with you, the only way to begin to reclaim your fullness of joy is to retract from the connection to the degree that circumstances permit, or completely. Joy is the protective attribute of your soul. Listen.

3. **Transmitting to others.** In order to maintain your primary connection with your Joy Source, it is necessary to remain unattached to the outcome when sending a BFE to others. Observe the quality of the response, or perhaps nonresponse. If your BFE is accepted, be aware of how the quality of the connection develops. Be aware of imbalances, like the tendency to focus on trying to change others or force issues. For joyful connection, mutual respect, integrity, and understanding are required.

Now that we have touched on some of the mystical and scientific elements of your baby spine and your relationship to it, we will begin blazing that inner trail that leads to the calmness, purity, and joy that is your true nature.

In the pages that follow, you will learn the Secret to recovering from exhaustion and how to move from energy deficit to well-being surplus. It is as near as your breath.

Daily Joy Reflection

What can I do today to cultivate a calm inner atmosphere?

CHAPTER 2

Ancient Secret #1
Pranayama – Vitality Control

For decades I suffered from existential angst. No matter how much I accomplished, I wasn't able to fully celebrate and enjoy those wins because I was far too concerned about others' approval. I had given my power away to external sources: the withholding bubble busters and carrot danglers. With them, approval was never attainable. One such win was when Paramount Studios chose me to create a yoga video for the internationally distributed *Buns of Steel* label. With this win, and any effort to excel, I discovered that not everyone is comfortable with people who enjoy moving and expanding to broader horizons. I experienced a variety of disappointing responses from neighbors, relatives, and so-called friends. Some began fawning to get money from me, assuming I was suddenly wealthy.

There were those who sneered, diminished, and called me "lucky," even though I began a disciplined meditation practice at the age of fourteen. Meanwhile, students and fans of the video shared the great benefits they received from the video, getting them "through cancer, deaths, and divorces." I joke, saying the "buns" catalyzed my career, opening doors for speaking engagements, teaching the military, university students, and hospitals, and even doing stand-up comedy at festivals. Yet, because of the few who felt threatened and were sabotaging, including family members, I tended to unconsciously diminish myself in order to belong.

Eventually, I realized that expressing my heart and soul fully and joyfully is a matter of health.

Once I discovered that breathing connected me to calmness, the foundation for joy, I knew I needed to make it a daily habit. I kept my vow to my five-year-old self that my life would not be like the old man on the porch full of blame and regret! Ugh! Breathing consciously eventually led me to impervious joy. It felt like an accidental discovery, but now I know it's a natural result of the Ancient Secrets taught by masters. I also discovered that joy is accessible regardless of others' opinions of me.

Breathing is the most underrated treasure that we have. We breathe unconsciously and usually only value this primary gift of life when a cold or respiratory condition hampers our breathing. Conscious breath is the portal to the peaceful paradise within. The ancient practice of pranayama (conscious breathing for vitality control) is the link to passionate, pleasurable meditation.

Your Greatest ROI

When you consider the vitality of life as your currency, there is no greater return on investment (ROI) than pranayama. The ancient Sanskrit word *prana* translates to vitality and *yama* means control. By taking time daily for pranayama, you will maintain balance in your vitality account. When your vitality account is overdrawn and deficient from engaging habitually with draining connections, joy feels lost. With pranayama, you can penetrate the layers of mental restlessness and reclaim your joy connection. Regular practice of pranayama has a cumulative effect, resulting in a surplus of vitality. This creates prime conditions for joy to saturate your inner atmosphere, the space within your skin.

With this Secret, you can master the currency of your vitality flow by using conscious breathing, the connecting link between your body, mind, and Joy Source. Pranayama is the practice of conducting the fuel flow that sustains your body. This is why it is primary. Conscious breathing is the quickest route to embodying joy, to having the experience of joy that is not contingent on circumstances.

The consistent results of calm physical ease and embodied joy from pranayama will become a daily habit that you will look forward to. It is a portable pleasure. Once you've established your mind-body connection to joy, you have access to increasing calmness, mental clarity, creativity, solutions, keen intuition, emotional balance, and health. It is for this reason that great masters are repetitious about the importance of simplicity.

Simplify for Joy's Sake

Living a chaotic life creates layers of muck over our beautiful, pure Joy Source, fraying the nerves. The time and energy required to return to calmness are commensurate with the level of chaos we live in. Chaos requires reserves of vitality to settle down into a calm, balanced state of being. With a simple, peaceful, flowing, loving lifestyle, a state of calmness can prevail in our nervous system throughout the day. With that established tone of embodied calmness, there is less noise to work through to feel joy. Simplicity allows for a quick and ever deepening connection to the replenishing surplus in your vitality account.

In order to increase simplicity and maintain a balance, it's important to settle all accounts with others (our external BFEs, whether broadcast or received). Whether another is violating us, or perhaps we are the ones who are extending unhealthy BFEs, this is imbalance. If this is the case, an inner or spoken forgiveness is in order, or sometimes an external action like calling the police is required for settling accounts. Every situation is different, yet pranayama (conscious breathing) consistently leads to calmness, clarity, and intuitive solutions for balance. The solution may be one of action or nonaction. Intuition operates case by case, not as a one size fits all.

Somewhere in my travels, I saw a bumper sticker that read, "Don't get even, get odd." Intuitive guidance feels like that because it comes from beyond the regurgitating intellect. The inner guidance may feel very odd, but it is never vindictive.

This truly sums up the funny guidance I receive from my gut. The solutions are always a combination of purity of heart, boldness, and ingenuity. There can also be calm ferocity, righteous anger, and even playfulness, but never bitterness. It can take time to develop trust in your Joy Source, but with a few successes under your belt or a history of success, you will stop wasting time second-guessing yourself. You can start with small things in listening to your intuition, for instance, what to order from a menu or where to shop and finding the perfect item at the perfect price. Take a breath, calm yourself, and ask and listen.

Your mind will often give you contrary information, claiming that you should do what you did yesterday or trying to talk you into taking a lazy route. I've made that mistake. Following my intuition led me to a beautiful flowing experience filled with abundant surprises the day before, so my reasoning mind would argue that I should do the same thing today. It doesn't work that way. When I overrode the guidance of the *new* day, it didn't have the same flow as yesterday's, and it even led to disappointment.

In the state of pure being, the answers click like Cupid's arrow, a pierce to the heart. Intuition is always accessible; it's our responsibility to connect to it. I have numerous stories of following through on oddball intuition and shaking my head at the amazingly favorable results.

Another important distinguishing point is that intuition does not lead to reactive, unconscious flying off the handle but rather calm, knowing responses backed by reason. Calm knowing combined with your purity of joy makes it easy to self-righteously stand up for yourself and boldly set boundaries. No matter the circumstances or appearances in your life, through pranayama you will know that within you is a steady, stable place of joy—as near as your breath. There is no better ROI than that.

With the thought of slowing down to breathe consciously, many people's first response is "I don't have time to meditate on breathing." It's considered a chore, like a burden. You don't have time to meditate? Pay me; I'll do it for you. Sorry, it doesn't work that way. I'd be wealthy beyond measure if it did. With the simplicity of the Transition Breath, the pranayama meditation hack below, you will begin to discover the unlimited capacity for pleasure, well-being, clear intuition, the discovery of ever greater awareness, and ultimately self-mastery! These are just some of the reasons that meditation is my greatest passion.

Mini Meditation Hack – Transition Breath

While you can receive all the well-wishing in the world from others, only you are responsible for maintaining your connection to your Joy Source. If this level of accountability feels daunting, here's some encouraging news, you can become as addicted to the blissful states of calmness as you can to the biochemical addictions of drama and chaos. Take your pick. To this day, I occasionally have a whirlwind of activity that leads my ego to believe that I don't have time to meditate, which ironically is when I need it most.

To get myself into the habit, I created the Transition Breath to trick myself out of my ego and into my Joy Source. For those with the common lack-of-time excuse, begin developing the habit by committing to one cycle of breath per day, just once a day. Then, gradually add breathing cycles into your day between activities. This is a simple way to assimilate what you have just completed and to breathe consciously in preparation for your next move. By doing this, you are signaling calmness and love to your nervous system. With the Transition Breath, you will increase present-mindedness and calm efficiency while minimizing absentmindedness and clumsiness.

As happens with me and my clients, the pleasant results of one cycle of the Transition Breath often lead to another, and suddenly you're connected to your Joy Source. To support your breathing habit, make a note of it in your planner for each day.

Don't concern yourself about dropping unhealthy habits to do meditation. Instead, focus on including the Transition Breath into your days. And don't be surprised if the appealing calmness, clarity, and well-being you start to experience cause you to lose interest in the unhealthy habits. This is how I developed my passion for meditation; the effort turned into a joyfully anticipated habit. The states of joy that result from the Secrets are distinctly different from the raging hormones that scream for fleeting pleasures. The connection to infinite Joy Source deepens with every BFE here and can even lead to states of bliss. These states are not contingent on anyone or anything outside of us. Meditation—the new orgasm!

Transition Breath

Inhale five counts. Retain five counts. Exhale five counts. Pause five counts. Tailor the count duration and intervals to feel as natural and pleasurable as possible. You'll begin to develop positive associations with slowing down and deepening your connection to peace, the predecessor to joy.

After you've mastered applying the Transition Breath between activities daily, begin adding one more cycle each day. You'll find yourself stepping forward with a calm presence, ready to joyfully embrace each activity. When you catch yourself slipping into anxiety, you can exhale softly and pause, drop your shoulders, and relax your belly anytime, anywhere.

Caution! If your lungs are not used to this depth of oxygenation, you may get dizzy, so do not do it while driving.

Divine Pause in Stillness

This point in the cycle of breath—the pause, momentarily not breathing—is a powerful moment to deepen self-mastery. Mystically, while in the stillness of the pause, keen awareness, beautiful insights, creativity, and solutions pop like light bulbs. Scientifically, you calm your nerves into a peace beyond understanding, ease saturates your inner atmosphere, and muscles relax.

Remain in the calm, breathless space of stillness as long as it feels natural while diving deeper into your heart and soul. Here is where you connect to the pure substance of life in your baby spine, fortifying the beautiful light of your Soul Wall. With regular visits to your Joy Source, your connection deepens, and the light of your Soul Wall expands. Feeling the stillness within your own inner atmosphere becomes such a pleasurable place that you will gradually lose interest in detrimental habits. In the stillness, nothing in mankind's creation can compare. You will find yourself intuitively moving away from chaos and dwelling in beauty, peace, and goodness. Your outer atmosphere will increasingly match the beauty of your inner atmosphere.

Summoning Presence

In the divine pause, you can summon yourself into presence by repeating an affirmative word or phrase. Experiment with words that work for you. Be creative. To summon my presence into the moment, I affirm the words "right here, right here, right here" with each soft exhale. I feel my eyes softening inward. If your mind wanders, resume the counting. Counting helps you maintain presence. When the pauses spontaneously lengthen, it may feel startling, yet this is a sacred stillness for feeling deeply present right here in the moment. Know that when you deeply calm your nervous system, stillness of breath becomes a natural state. This is the opposite of a panting, gasping, stress-ridden breath that results from an overstimulated and restless nervous system. Life happens every day, so doing pranayama every day is of great benefit. Affirm spoken words, softly whispered or silently, and eventually feel your pure presence *right here.*

Please note that the Transition Breath ratio is a basic place to begin. Of course, the way you are breathing is never to be judged but observed. Let your breathing inform you of the state of your emotions. With this self-awareness, you can compassionately face and breathe through whatever is revealed to you. Developing awareness of your own breathing patterns will also enable you to identify the inner state of others by observing their breathing. This will assist you in your social discernment, understanding, and harmonious interactions.

Now that you have the primary Secret that blazes and clears the trail to calmness, you can add the next Secret for embodying joy. You will now go beyond thinking of joy as an intellectual concept to experiencing it and becoming comfortable in your own skin.

Fierce Joy Action
Menu Secret #1

- Enjoy the portable pleasure of conscious breathing daily.
- Observe the quality of your breathing for self-awareness and understanding others.
- For enhanced well-being, feel gratitude while you are breathing.
- When your mind wanders during pranayama (vitality control), return to counting.
- As lung capacity increases, alter the intervals and play with the ratios.
- Begin doing a cycle of the Transition Breath between activities.
- Summon your presence regularly by combining breath with affirming "right here."
- Let each breath be a devotional love offering to your Joy Source within.
- Softly exhale while affirming intentions and calm efficiency before you go out the door.

Daily Joy Reflection

What can I do today to simplify my life?

CHAPTER 3

Ancient Secret #2

Pratyahara – Turn Senses Inward

The external noise of the world, the incessant bombardment of others' opinions, and the pressures and the lure of external pleasures can make it difficult to feel the quiet, gradual transformation that occurs as you live the Secrets. My own transformation eventually became apparent, so much so that people repeatedly told me, "You seem so comfortable in your own skin." But this was not always the case, not by a long shot. I literally lived life with sweaty palms for decades, a result of anxiety. If this is the case for you, be grateful for the self-awareness. These physical symptoms are informing you. After learning to live from continuity of peace and fierce joy, my hands stopped sweating.

With the Ancient Secret, pratyahara (turning senses inward), you can reclaim your energy from the depleting connections you've established with external situations, as mentioned above. In a state of calmness, imagine the BFEs that you've transmitted outwardly as tendrils, or perhaps as ribbons. To turn your senses inward, feel as though you are reeling those tendrils of energy back to your inner atmosphere. Observe the quality of the BFEs and let yourself be informed by what you discover. Notice the connections between your thoughts, emotions, and sensations. Pratyahara is the way to move through the doorways of the five physical senses to begin fully embodying the space within your own skin. After turning the senses inward, you can begin cultivating a peaceful, pleasurable place to inhabit. This will establish the foundation for connecting with Joy Source.

Keep going, finding the simple pleasure of being *right here* with this breath. The benefits are immediate and have a cumulative physical effect. Our culture uses language that perpetuates a spin on reducing *anxiety and stress* rather than increasing *ease and well-being*. The Secrets emphasize focus on the latter. The old saying goes, "It was the last straw that broke the camel's back," implying that one little pressure after another eventually leads to a person hitting a threshold of anger, frustration, or worse. By the same token, a breath can seem like a small, inconsequential thing; however, a dedicated practice of conscious breathing will annihilate the adverse effects of one too many straws while creating a surplus of ease and well-being.

With my well-earned baseline of calmness, I now more quickly foresee potential "last straws" and determinedly apply the Secrets. If you slip into imbalance, you can always return to your Joy Source.

Embodying Your Inner Atmosphere

One final last straw, which undeniably informed me that I was not comfortable within my own skin, was when I began to suffer from eczema on my face. It's an inflammatory itchy skin condition. This body signal vehemently called me to pay attention to how I felt within my own skin, and I had no choice but to face it; every time I looked in the mirror, I saw it. With the Secrets, I got to the bottom of this skin condition.

During this time, I was dating a man who was fun, kind, and generous most of the time; however, he cyclically raged, flying off the handle. This is when I got a clue! When his temper would flare, my skin would flare. Hello! While he seemed relieved in dumping his miserable mood, my skin would immediately become uncomfortable and itchy. The correlation was in my face and on my face, so I dug deeper. Why would I even bother spending time with an emotionally unstable person? The painful truth was that it was familiar. I had a grandmother who cyclically raged. You could count on it at every family gathering. She threw tantrums like a two-year-old: yelling, stomping out, and slamming doors. As a kid, I felt perplexed, wondering if anybody else noticed this insanity, but the grown-ups sat stiffly, intimidated, accepting this outlandish behavior year after year, decade after decade.

As is the case with dysfunctional families, I received the unspoken message that this is normal. Eventually, as an adult, I made the decision to pass on going to family gatherings where this raging, tortured soul attended.

Frankly, I did not miss her, not one bit. I went through a period of grieving the death of my fantasy of her becoming a kind, gentle grandmother, but the joy and freedom I felt far surpassed the shattered illusion. In fact, after this experience, I acquired a taste of the freedom that results from facing truth. This single choice revolutionized my life. I do not take responsibility for anybody's moods. People who rage and fly off the handle display a red flag warning that I unflinchingly take heed of. They are simply not allowed in my personal world, biologically related or not.

This was the beginning of what I call doing my archeological digs. I dug deep in search of the buried fossils, the causes of dis-ease, and the disruption of my well-being. The discoveries aren't always pretty or pleasant but are well worth unearthing. Bringing the causes to the surface of my awareness was emotionally painful, but ultimately freeing. Underneath the bedrock of anxiety and dis-ease is where I found the source of impervious joy, deep within the purity of my baby spine.

I discovered that reconnecting here is as near as the breath, and I return daily to replenish vitality and restore ease. This is the reward of the archeological dig. I've done a few excavations since and seek the priceless buried treasures with joyful anticipation because I know the resulting freedom. Like any archaeological expedition, there is a beginning and an end. After you discover the treasures of self-awareness, you're free to move on with your new, bolder way of being. Now I ask, "How much ease and well-being am I capable of experiencing within my own skin?"

Begin tracking new physical sensations. Pause and ask, "What was I just thinking when I felt that sensation?" Identify the thought. The life-giving, pleasurable sensations will increase as you focus on truth and beauty, even the painful truth.

When you get into the swing of doing the Transition Breath, finding the pleasure of it, and increasing the number of cycles, you will begin to move into a closer connection with your Joy Source. With each cycle, the connection between mind and body deepens. It's natural to feel the tensions in your body as you move from the intellectual *thought* of calmness and joy to the *embodiment* of these qualities. As part of your baby spine care, observe and identify the physical sensations that are signaling for your attention. Acknowledge these invaluable signals, which always point you to *homeostasis*, the medical term for your body's natural desire to be in balance. Honoring the signals of homeostasis—the sensations—is a doorway to your intuition. Breathing into and through the sensations with care and compassion will show you what needs balancing in your inner atmosphere and who or what from your outer atmosphere contributes to imbalance.

There are amusing things to observe about our level of presence, catching how we might vocally agree to something, yet our nose wrinkles with distaste, revealing the truth of how we feel. Observing the direction of the feet can reveal whether a person is fully present or fragmented and scattered, with the mind going in one direction and the body another.

Embodiment Check-In Hack

What am I doing with my feet?
How am I breathing?
Can I drop my shoulders?
Can I relax my belly?
Can I quiet the movement of my eyes?
Can I soften my mouth and relax my jaw?
What thought patterns are creating physical tension?
What thought patterns are creating physical ease?
How is my body craving to move, stretch, walk, run, dance ... ?

Show interest in the informative sensations, just as a loving parent would show concern for how their child is feeling. Explore to identify and name the sensations. For instance, identify knots in the stomach, headaches, muscle tightness, clenched jaw, furrowed brow, and even the slightest ache or pain so that you can tend to these imbalances and breathe consciously to free yourself into physical ease.

Embodied journaling is a powerful tool for seeing the interconnectedness between the emotions, thoughts, and sensations playing out within your skin. As you journal about your experiences and interactions, observe your physical sensations, facial expressions, vibrations, and emotional reactions and write about them too. You will find the flow of your pen moving differently with your varied emotions. For your own awareness and understanding, identify peaceful writing, angry writing, tender writing, funny writing, perplexed writing, reviewing-events writing, business writing, and every kind of writing.

Whatever you do, don't edit yourself. You are revealing yourself to yourself. Just as the sun shines on everyone, let the light of awareness shine on all facets of yourself. This will be your tracking system to become more caring and mindful about your choices, what and who brings you joy, and who drains it. Just as you can catch, address, and tend to the signals of imbalance, you can be informed by physical sensations of ease, like a calm heart, soft eyes, a thought pattern, or memories that bring radiant warmth to your heart or a smile to your face. You might write about something that moves you to growl, laugh out loud, pump your fist, or spontaneously do a happy dance.

While the five physical senses signal both pleasure and pain, awareness of them is a great key to the doorway into presence. After you've crossed the threshold into presence, you can more easily recognize the relationship between your thoughts, emotions, and sensations and begin connecting more deeply to your Joy Source.

The state of joy is distinctly different from passing sensations and fluctuating emotions. We are not meant to be slaves to the senses; rather, they are to serve our joy. Joy is the nature of your soul. It's ever present, renewing, and refreshing.

Harsh memories may make your body cringe, but they offer an opportunity to remember a lesson learned so as to avoid repeating it—or to forgive yourself. Forgiveness brings great physical ease. Because some new awarenesses are extremely painful to face, you set your own pace. Give yourself grace and compassion as you sort through revelations of shattered dreams or fantasies that must be grieved, released, and blessed into the past.

While these are all part of being human, going through the involved emotions can physically feel like you've been hit by a Mack truck. Plenty of rest and additional naps are a natural and healthy response to moving through this emotional hangover. The pleasant, pleasurable sensations of a beautiful memory set tones of ease and well-being. We feel a spectrum of emotions, wobbling between an undercurrent of anxiety and physical ease. The Ancient Secrets blaze the trail to *continuity* of embodied ease, and you find yourself dwelling in harmony within your own skin.

As you've probably gathered, the Ancient Secrets are a matter of health! In fact, research shows that 80 percent of all doctor's appointments are made for stress-related conditions. In mankind's creation, psychological stress issues are called human nature and natural states, but these are altered states from our true nature, the state of joy. With the Secrets, you can be that one out of five people who masters their well-being. You get to be in charge of making your inner atmosphere a pleasurable place to be.

Breathe, listen, and gather inward to the voice of life, your natural joy state.

As you learn to value and deepen your Joy Source connection, it will become natural to want to prioritize that connection above all others. You'll reel in the energy sent out to BFEs that are fruitlessly dangling out there, leaking, draining, or sucking the life out of you. Setting fierce boundaries to maintain your joy connection will become as natural as a loving parent automatically protecting their beloved child.

After identifying your embodied sensations, the next Ancient Secret, swadhyaya (self-inquiry), will help you identify to whom or what is causing your joy to leak. This could be your own beliefs or others' limited projections of you. With the great treasure of self-awareness that results from self-inquiry, you will know where the draining energy leaks are coming from and reclaim your joy, your birthright. As a practicing master of the Ancient Secrets, you'll eventually graduate to continuity of embodied fierce joy. You will be able to move adeptly from the need to *reclaim* your joy to *maintaining* your joy and eventually *roaring* with fierce, impervious joy.

Fierce Joy Action
Menu Secret #2

- Enjoy movement that feels good, and breathe yourself deeper into the pleasure.
- Identify the pleasurable sensations as you strengthen your body's muscles and systems.
- To summon your presence, occasionally ask, "What am I doing with my feet?"
- Take time to rest after unearthing deeply buried emotions in archeological digs.
- Enjoy the mood-elevating joy endorphins that increase as you exercise with pleasure.
- Enjoy movement that relieves stiffness from muscles and connective tissue.
- Simultaneously feel and think thoughts that affirm your wholeness as you move.
- Release sound as you move to enhance the pleasure or growl out frustrations.
- Use movement to express the self-awareness gleaned from your embodied writing.

Daily Joy Reflection

What can I do today to take care of my health?

CHAPTER 4

Ancient Secret #3
Swadhyaya – Self-Inquiry

Just before Paramount Studios called to interview me about creating the *Buns of Steel Yoga* video, I was dating a man with whom I had everything in common. We enjoyed hiking, biking, meditating, cooking, laughing, and dancing together. It didn't hurt that I thought he was hot looking. But I was puzzled because I always felt deflated, coming away second-guessing my choices after spending time with him. I felt duped. As I began to observe our interactions and reflect, I began to get a clue. It appeared that anything that brought me joy, he would make a diminishing comment about it. In fact, he would make a campaign of it. At that time, I was enjoying my professional dance training classes, some ballet, jazz, African, modern, and hip-hop. One time he showed up at the dance studio, glaring at me with his eyes narrowed to little slits, as though I was doing something shameful. Later, he commented about how selfish dancers are for watching themselves in the mirror. I was so conditioned to seek approval that I actually took his comment to heart and considered it. Over the few months together, I felt my joy and confidence draining.

Even though the masters warned me, I did not want to face the fact that some aspects of human nature could be so treacherous. I knew my spirit would not survive if I continued interacting with this man. To double-check my suspicions, I put him to the test. I was living in Los Angeles at the time and was curious about the ministry classes taught by the best-selling author and great mystic, Michael Bernard Beckwith. I eagerly signed up for his foundation classes. Feeling great joyful anticipation, I purposely shared my plans with the joy robber I was dating to test his reaction. Get your popcorn buttered; you probably don't need a spoiler alert! Like a boring, predictable movie plot, he launched into his campaign of diminishing remarks: "Why would you do that?" "I heard this . . ." "I heard that about . . ." (Fill in the derogatory remarks.) My suspicions were confirmed. This joy robber was systematically chipping away at my spirit. While I did feel a strong connection with the former boyfriend, I accepted that he wasn't good for me and moved on. Mind you, I also endured female "friends" who were discrediting and diminishing. Joy robbers do not exclude gender. With these glaring patterns, I was again motivated to do an archaeological dig to unearth what brought me to align with such malevolent forces.

I took the opportunity to put into practice what the great masters told me, and it works:

When someone doesn't want to come into balance with you, immediately release them. You will be surprised how quickly the countless gifts of life begin to flow to you.

I went on to complete all the foundation classes with Beckwith and enjoyed every minute of the studies, unfettered and free of the joy robber. I also returned to my dance classes with more joyful abandon than ever!

Shortly after the breakup, I began having visions of doing a yoga video, which my mind and pocketbook couldn't conceive of, but the vision persisted. It was like some cosmic orchestration was going on. Suddenly people were coming to me from out of the blue saying, "You should do a video." Plus, the focus and support I received in the foundational ministry classes with Beckwith fueled the vision. The vision emerged from my Joy Source within, and my celestial light buddies were apparently sending people-messengers to encourage me.

Finally, after accepting that a yoga video would somehow come through me to be fulfilled, I began to affirm daily and visualized the benefit the video would have on my viewers. Paramount Studios called me two months after I began the affirming and visualizing. A talent scout had heard about my yoga classes and chose me to create a yoga video for their mind-body series. To an outsider, it would appear that the call from Paramount Studios was random, but I foresaw it, people suggested it, I affirmed it, and I began visualizing the vision. For this reason, being chosen was anticlimactic; it felt to me like, "Here it is. I've been preparing for this. Let's get going."

The vision was fulfilled without paying a dime from my own pocketbook. To top it off, I got to share the journey of the yoga video with my class. During my graduation presentation on the stage of Agape International, I playfully turned around to show the class what "qualified" me for the "buns" video. My class shared laughter and applause, including one of the greatest joy bringers I've ever known, Michael Bernard Beckwith.

During this time, I was also collaborating with songwriters and sang some lyrics to the crowd, "The truest love is the most unknown. It goes far beyond fear of being alone." The lyrics and melody are an earworm to this day. It was a glorious graduation ceremony of joyful fulfillment.

I'm grateful for the powerful principle that great masters taught me. When someone does not want to come into balance with you, immediately let them go. Even though breaking up was momentarily sad, I'd followed the masters' guidance, removing myself from a joy robber and redirecting myself to joy bringers.

By developing the habit of checking the quality of your BFEs, rooting out and releasing joy robbers, you will clear the way for meaningful, peaceful, flowing, loving experiences. This is how you create the joy lifestyle. Go easy on yourself. My transition from being a chronic people-pleasing doormat to a boldly confident entertainer took years; years of shaking, sweating, and letting go of unnecessary guilt for enjoying my birthright. Keep going. You, too, will roar with fierce joy.

Know Thyself, Enjoy Thyself

The Ancient Secret of swadhyaya (self-inquiry) reveals not only joy robbers in the external environment, but the joy-robbing thoughts and attitudes that we cultivate in our own inner atmosphere, the space within our skin. From this Secret, I derive empowering delight in knowing I get to choose the thoughts that increase my embodied joy capacity. By knowing I am sovereign over my inner atmosphere, I am less vulnerable to others' fabricated views of me. From this honest assessment, I come to *know myself*. As I know myself, I can more readily *be myself*. Then, I am able to fully *enjoy being myself*. This is the result I have received from the Secrets. I enjoy being me.

With this self-knowledge, you will gain a deeper understanding of human nature. You will become so proficient at determining the quality of BFEs, transmitted from you or to you, that you'll begin making wise choices daily. For those BFEs broadcast to you from others, you'll begin to know the potential results in advance. The predictability enables you to then discern to what degree you will respond to, ignore, or flat out reject the BFEs. For the approval-seeking addict, acting on your own behalf will initially feel selfish, perhaps even scary. Maintaining joy will feel unnatural at first. After second-guessing yourself for so long, you will question, "Am I allowed to feel so much well-being?" Yes! Instead, ask yourself, "How much well-being can I stand? Where are the limits? Who puts the limits on me?"

But like any addiction recovery, there is the painful process of withdrawal. If you are in the vulnerable position of being dependent on a joy robber, secretly planning your escape is advisable. Those who are used to stealing your beautiful radiance and walking on you like a doormat will predictably escalate oppressive, diminishing tactics. Again, get your popcorn buttered—as you're throwing your sheets out the window.

Knowing your true nature and fully enjoying being you anchors you to Joy Source. This gives you immunity to a world full of draining diversions, distractions, illusions, bombarding media, and miserable trolls. Realizing the danger of approval-seeking, you will feel relief by accepting that not everyone likes you or wants to be around you. The ease you will feel from acceptance sets the stage for joy, and joy is the protective attribute of the soul. A person who is free, who doesn't give a flying hoot what others think of them, is disturbing to those who are chronically miserable or too lazy to be accountable for their own moods. They are filled with oppressive dogmatic limitations; their joy nature is deeply buried under the mud of deluded cultural beliefs.

If my freedom in joy disturbs another's dogma, I am more than happy to free them of their discomfort and steer clear of those moody joy robbers. If my joy disturbs others, toodle-oo! They can like it or lump it. So, let's dig in. Snap out of the worry trance of the approval-seeking habit. Seek first your true nature: joy. Look forward to feeling that internal current within your own skin.

Dense Human Nature

It's clearly evident that mankind is not only repetitious but predictable. Just read any viable history book. Check out the news, law cases, therapy research, and common family dysfunction; substance, emotional, psychological, and physical abuse; suicide, homicide, investigative reports; local and global corruption; and the patterns of human nature become tiresome, if not downright boring. The dense human animal nature is distinguishably different from our true joy nature. Joy is a state of being, not an emotion. The predictable gifts from our innate Joy Source are always fresh, wholesome surprises and of benefit to self and others—never boring. The Secrets result in an ever-deepening connection to joy, right here, within your own skin. Masters taught about the four basic densities: doubt, fear, selfishness, and greed. These ingredients are the murky mud covering the soul's magnificent radiance. The Secrets clear away the mud to reveal your natural radiance.

Formality Cures Overfamiliarity

Familiarity breeds contempt. It's common human behavior to fall into patterns of disrespect, disdain, and, worse, taking others for granted. This occurs throughout all types of relationships, from business to biological family. This behavior especially causes deep suffering between spouses and family members to whom we've opened our hearts. Our culture feeds the dangerously dysfunctional notion that family should stick together no matter what. It is a sweet notion, but it can be especially devastating to experience betrayal from family members.

After vowing never to expose myself to my cruel biological grandmother, one of my first joy robbers, I fortuitously met an elder who playfully announced, "You're my kid." Ann spoke only affirmative words to me, nurturing my spirit, and repeatedly told me, "Never underestimate the value of what you are sharing with people in your service." She'd correct me like a fierce mama bear if I ever spoke about myself in a diminishing way. She'd express contrasting uplifting words to nullify my limiting words. This was the grandmother I'd always longed for.

Ann's love filled and healed all the places my biological grandmother had shredded. It sometimes takes courage, but trust that the joy robbers can be replaced. I had prayed for a new grandmother for seven years. The tears I had cried over the death of a fantasy transformed into joy tears of gratitude when I realized that Ann was the answer to my prayers. Beloved Ann has since passed away, yet I smile and feel eternal joy for having known her.

In order for me to move forward, it was necessary to cut off ties with my oppressive, toxic grandmother. Being an extreme joy robber, she wasn't safe to be around with her incessant expressions of disdain and contempt. I never put myself in her presence again, and it was the right decision. I began to feel a continuity of joy and forward momentum. After freeing myself of a fantasy that never came true, I imagined how I would feel with the nurturing support of a kind grandmother. With beloved Ann, I experienced the beautiful difference between fantasy and imagination.

When others slip into disrespectful *overfamiliarity*, I treat them with *reserved formality*. This is a useful tactic for establishing your demeanor of self-respect while relaying the unspoken message that there's no room for argument. Because Ann was consistently kind and respectful to me, it was safe for me to generously extend my warmth to her. There was nothing to prove and no approval to seek. She generously gave me love and support.

With this choice of replacing my grandmother, I unconsciously set a standard for myself about the quality of *all* my relationships, with a surprising side effect. After choosing to value my peace over a joy-robbing relative, I began immediately identifying all joy robbers, related or not. They are simply not allowed into my personal world. Now I am maintaining continuity of joy and continuity of peace as the masters taught me to. Try it. Be formal and reserved with those who are disrespectful.

Elegance of Discipline

Dense, unmanaged emotions lead to clumsy, rash, compulsiveness, absentmindedness, self-sabotage, or harmfulness to self and others. In one word: chaos. Imagine the meaning of the old saying, "Like a bull in a China shop." A huge wild beast in small aisles of delicate dinnerware. This is generally the atmosphere of joy robbers, recklessly and insensitively stampeding over others. In mankind's loony-bin creation, it requires immense discipline to maintain joy. Joy robbers lack that discipline. They'd rather steal it from others and even get some perverse pleasure out of seeing others down.

As you increase your self-mastery, you'll begin to view the tiresome joy robbers as overgrown, lazy, undisciplined, immature children. Your daily discipline with the Secrets will assist you in catching your own joy-robbing thoughts. You may even shake your head and laugh at your own human pettiness in light of your increasing self-awareness. Your Joy Source will always lead you to gracious, harmonious, balanced, elegant choices.

With the incessant distractions of social media, attention spans have drastically shortened. The ability to focus for extended periods of time is now the new advantage. Darting eyes, anxiety, depression, impatience, and shallow breathing are all symptoms of internal chaos. To develop focus, a commitment to discipline is absolutely necessary. To increase my ability to focus on projects for extensive periods of time, I began setting my phone alarm to dedicate a particular number of hours to the task. It took some practice, but I eventually developed the habit of focus. It's such a refreshing feeling to get into a flow and thoroughly complete a task without interruption.

The ability to focus is transferrable to all areas of life, not just work and exercise but also committing one hundred percent to everything, be it deeply listening to others, breathing consciously, fully resting, reflection time, even do-nothing time. Discipline for developing focus will result in moving through the world with calm efficiency. Living this way, summoning all of your energy into what you're doing, makes each moment supremely rich and satisfying. Spending time with those who share these values leads to peaceful, flowing, loving experiences together.

Inner and Outer Atmosphere Cleanse

When others project their diminishing view onto you, your intuition will be the best guide for the degree you allow them into your personal world. This is a negative BFE being transmitted to you. Day by day, case by case, by inquiring with your Joy Source, you will be given the steps for removing yourself as graciously, safely, and proactively as possible. Challenges with others represent the beautiful lessons we need to learn to love, value, and respect our Joy Source above all! Sometimes a joy robber's toxicity is so clearly dangerous that we must immediately remove ourselves from their presence. The murky thoughts and energies people project about each other do not stay inside their heads. An example of this is how people on social media can strike up an energy connection with someone in another country whom they've never met. The mutual BFEs get intertwined, engaged, and enmeshed. Energy travels. This is why the Secrets are useful for daily cleansing.

Making a lifestyle of the Ancient Secrets will lead you to make choices from calmness and clarity, taking you out of the confusion of illusion. Your intuition, that beautiful faculty of your soul, will become so keen that you will sense in advance when a person is not in harmony with your joy.

This will help prevent you from lingering in time-wasting interactions. You will preserve your precious vitality of life to invest in fruitful, meaningful, fun directions.

Knowing that energy travels, I free everyone else from my mind daily, sending Soul Wall boundaries to joy robbers and love to all. I affirm that I am free daily. Everyone else is free. I broadcast BFEs of fierce joy and love, and that's all that I allow in. Freeing yourself of projected densities is not done to feel superior but to be self-responsible. You get to be in charge of your thoughts and attitudes.

Cleanse and Reprogram

There are a number of techniques for cleansing murk off of your golden core of joy.

Below I offer three simple portable cleansing techniques:

1. **Quiver of Life** – Take a deep breath in, stretch, and simultaneously tense every muscle of your body until you quiver. Isometrically squeeze out the densities. As you quiver, think your chosen affirmation. The idea is to feel as though you are squeezing out all densities and replacing them with a good feeling quality. Examples would be "Only love is allowed in this body," "The energy and power of the Universe is saturating every fiber, cell, bone, and tissue of my body temple," and "I command my mind to calmness and clarity." Have fun creating your own programming menus.

The beauty of the Quiver of life technique is that you can be on a walk, anywhere, and look like you're just enjoying a good stretch.

2. **Shower Cleanse** – Consciously focus on water flowing on the areas of unease, visualizing the densities going down the drain to be purified like fresh spring waters. Generally, I focus on relaxing the muscles with warm water and cool temperatures for cleansing the dense BFEs that glom on to different areas. Affirm all clingers, attachments, drainers, and grippies off and out!

By all means, purify from head to toe, daily. Keep it fresh. Reveal your beautiful, sparkling fierce joy vibes!

3. **Side Stance** – This is more of a preemptive technique than a cleansing one. It will assist in minimizing draining connections from glomming on to you. When you are in the presence of a joy robber, avoid having your body face fully forward. This is where the term "cold shoulder" comes from. Consider the opposite. When you feel complete safety, trust, and support with a friend, you not only fully face them, you joyfully hug and embrace each other. Being physically wide open with a joy robber is like willingly putting your head on a chopping block; it's masochistic and self-victimizing. A side stance will help prevent joy robber's low-intention vibrations from penetrating the major energy centers of your body.

Self-Honesty – An Acquired Taste

Sometimes we're so attached to wishful thinking, a fantasy, that facing the facts is too painful. We all need grace to go at our own pace. But to steadily move forward, shattering illusions is necessary. The longer we dwell in a dead-end fantasy, the further we move away from our fierce joy and the more work it will take to return to ourselves. Self-inquiry, the Ancient Secret of swadhyaya, assists in being aware enough to make wise choices and curtail tendencies to be a joy robber or to be robbed.

Feeling emotions as they surface sets them free. Otherwise, they remain as physical discomforts, which distract from joy. If hurts have been deeply buried, grieving can feel like a bottomless pit. Acknowledging painful emotions does not diminish your core of joy. Joy is a state of being, not an emotion. Unlike your Joy Source, emotions fluctuate. They come and go. Being present with painful emotions engenders thoughtful responses, while denial can lead to destructive emotional reactions. Eventually, tears of sorrow are replaced with tears full of the richness of life. To fully integrate the prolific beauty you are beginning to perceive and experience, you might need some extra solitude.

For deeply painful new awareness, two years is scant time to grieve for healing. The Ancient Secret of self-inquiry is like doing an archeological dig for the fossilized emotional secrets you've hidden from yourself. Like a literal archeological dig, after the crew leaves no stone unturned and the expedition is complete, you can celebrate your fascinating finds and move forward. You will feel an increase in lung capacity, breathing with greater ease. Eventually, discovering your self-imposed, limiting thought formations and others' projections starts to feel like a fun adventure!

As you build a history of success in self-mastery, facing the painful truth becomes an acquired taste. The contrast between mankind's spinning creation and your steady joy within reveals how illusory the external world is. Facing and uprooting limiting, painful patterns are how illusions get shattered. Yeah! Another illusion shattered is another step out of stagnation. Another illusion shattered is a cause for celebration; however, some grieving is also a natural part of this healing. Healing tears clear the way to forgiving yourself and others for dwelling in a fantasy. Grieve the fantasy. Repeatedly forgive yourself until you are set free to enjoy the unfolding alignment of joy in both your inner atmosphere and outer experiences.

Once you move through and release the pain, the awareness of your gifts, powers, and talents will become apparent. In your continuing self-inquiry, you'll become aware of the nuances of common blocks to owning and valuing your gifts, like fear of appearing arrogant, fear of others' jealousy, and competitive and sabotaging behaviors.

After reflecting in radical self-honesty, it can feel like an emotional hangover as you unearth buried parts of yourself. Take it easy on yourself. Meditation, conscious breathing, napping, affirming, silence, relaxed meals, and time in nature are all helpful for releasing the former ways and assimilating the new you. In this vital step, acknowledging and identifying your emotions without judgment is imperative. Denying embarrassing emotions is a form of self-suppression, which blocks joy. Those emotions will leak out in unconscious behaviors or result in a health condition. After identifying the natural spectrum of human emotions, choose a healthy outlet of expression. Awareness is always the first step toward conscious change.

Opinions Are Overrated – I Define Who I Am!

"NoMoreStay! MamaStay!" The cutie yoga kids I taught came up with all kinds of creative variations for the word namaste. They provided nonstop wild fun, exhausting, but fun! Of course, this included a lot of highbrow fart-related humor.

I had developed a yoga program for at-risk youth. It became an award-winning after-school enrichment program. This was when labeling and medicating children for ADD (attention deficit disorder) and ADHD (attention deficit hyperactivity disorder) were rampant. I learned that children from chaotic environments thrive with simple consistency. It makes them feel secure. We would repeat the same steps every time to establish order and mutual respect. And they did thrive in these conditions.

The first ten to fifteen minutes of the thirty-five-minute class were primarily used to get them in line before entering the room. Once that was established, I'd clearly state the next three steps: one, enter; two, remove shoes; three, sit. From there, one batch of five would be instructed to "walk, not run!" to a spot on the floor designated with a star. Every time a child slipped, we all started over until it occurred to them that they were holding back the entire class from moving forward to the fun part. Once settled, we'd close our eyes and do slow "balloon breathing" to identify feelings. Some examples they shared were "excited," "tired," "angry," "sad," and "happy."

Once they acknowledged their emotions, our yoga poses included the emotions each child shared. For example, we'd express with happy puppy moves, sad cow, angry tiger, and other variations to allow creative expression of their individual emotions. Every child felt seen, validated, and listened to as classmates and I mirrored their movements and feelings. At the end, they were happy to go into a final relaxation. They would return to slow, deep balloon belly breathing while I guided them on a visualization journey to a place where a treasure awaited them.

I'll never forget the look on their supervisors and teachers' faces the first time they walked in and saw all the children completely still. Their jaws dropped in shock and their eyes widened. I had simply taught the children the Ancient Secrets, which are transferrable to any age.

You know, I never saw ADD or ADHD. I saw little people, individual souls, children with vitality and energy, no different from myself at that age. For some reason, they seemed perfectly normal to me. As they implemented the

Secrets, they all experienced their Joy Source within while learning values and mutual respect toward others. As weeks progressed, they'd eagerly announce as soon as they saw me, "I have a feeling to share!" They felt safe doing so because they learned how to be self-aware and that they could calm themselves with conscious breathing. They experienced expressing emotions in a healthy way and enjoyed the grand finale of deep calmness within their own skins.

One of the most delightful and memorable experiences happened as we were ending a class. A little boy curled up into a fetal ball; his face was red, with an expression of utter disappointment. I asked what was wrong. He replied, "I want to share something with the class." I said, "Go ahead," and gestured for him to take the teaching platform. He quickly composed himself, took the stage, squared his shoulders, and confidently arranged himself in the tree pose, a balancing pose. Then the most amazing masterful tone of power boomed through the voice of his little body when he shared, "When your body is steady, your mind is steady." It was a satisfying moment for all.

The only glaringly painful part of this teaching experience was when the slow breathing calmed them; occasionally a child would weep. I'd quietly inquire, "Are you okay?" and sometimes the answer was quite tragic: "My brother was shot" or "My dad is in prison" . . . heartbreaking. Awareness arises in calmness. This is why some people would rather run with distractions; awareness can be painful. I was honored that the children felt safe enough to share with me. Their tears released some of the pain they'd been holding in their bodies, until they slowed down to relax and breathe. The little troopers would feel their emotions, express them, and then resume with playful participation.

These children enthusiastically explored the Ancient Secrets. During the thirty-five-minute class, they transcended the medical labels assigned to them by external authorities. Their example of fierce joy taught me that I am not anybody's opinion or label for me. I am not my passing emotions. I am not my experiences or circumstances.

From Approval Addict to Awareness Junkie

A female lieutenant was scouting for a yoga teacher for a local military base and chose me. It was quite ironic that I became the first yoga teacher in the military. Yet, I developed a feeling for all who were under my tutelage— as souls; ageless, genderless souls—who ultimately wanted to feel at peace within their own skins. When I taught yoga to the military, I heard they decided to shut down the Olympic-sized pool for two years. A young recruit died from exhaustion in the pool, trying to prove himself "man enough." Note that the word *prove* is a syllable of the word *approval.* The soldier was desperate for approval from an external authority.

Cultural conditioning to seek others' approval is rampant and potentially deadly! Minimally, giving anybody else authority over the desires of your intuitive soul makes you lose yourself, killing your spirit and your will to live. To the extreme, approval-seeking leads to death.

There are numerous stories about college students experiencing tragic results, even inadvertently killing themselves in a desperate attempt to fit in, dying to be liked. The college ritual of hazing sometimes goes to extremes. For example, requirements like jumping into a pool from rooftops or polishing off an inordinate amount of alcohol to be accepted into a club. The combination of peer pressure and a desire for approval will drown out the protective voice of intuition. Desiring and deepening connection to Joy Source, rather than external approval, is the antidote.

Also, beware of those who act as the "devil's advocate." There've been numerous times when devil's advocates have tried to discredit or minimize the seriousness of a matter, all after sharing that I felt something was off, meaning that my intuition was screaming for me to pay attention. They plant seeds of doubt, trying to get you to second-guess yourself, even after stating facts.

I've learned two things from my experience with those devil's advocates who try to convince me to see a different angle contrary to my intuitive knowing: One, I don't tell anyone my personal intuition in the moment; I *act* on it. My intuition leads me daily to the countless gifts of life, the right people, and safety. Two, I've observed that people who play devil's advocate live lives that sabotage their joy. They stay in unhealthy relationships and spin in dead-end circles.

After seeing me move forward in health, joy, and fulfillment, one devil's advocate said, "You did that so fast," referring to manifesting my goals. In my mind, I knew that I had simply followed the guidance from my Joy Source; I listened and implemented focused planning to come to that achievement. Devil's advocates are dangerous company. I've experienced their tactics of backstabbing, heartbreaking disloyalty, and sabotage in an effort to keep me held back with them. Let those who are advocates for the devil live with their devils.

Approval-seeking and ignoring your beautiful intuitive Joy Source can be deadly to your spirit and your body. Keep moving in your own direction. Quietly set forth into motion with fierce joy all that you build, remaining unfettered and free of the opinions of devil's advocates.

Grieving is Underrated

You may have noticed this happening in your own life, that after you've been in a cozy little rut, life will throw you a curveball. Suddenly, it's sink-or-swim time. Something happens that was not as you planned. The situation requires you to develop mental strength, determination, focus, and grit. If you avoid facing the challenge, you sink deeper and deeper into some nest of troubles.

We are not here to camp out on planet Earth. We're visiting. We're passing through. We are here for our education and entertainment, to continually grow, evolve, and enjoy every opportunity to attain self-mastery. As fulfilling as it is to develop in this way, it also means your old way of being (old comfortable habits and some relationships) needs to be changed or completely severed.

Embodying fierce joy, and the resulting balance, health, and goodness, means there's less room for densities in your life. Saying goodbye to unhealthy traits, harsh memories, and the associated people who you once felt close to can feel sad, nonetheless. At this stage, it is good to cry; it's right, it's natural, it's appropriate to cry. Emotions seek healing. Every little letting-go along the way is like a little death of the way things were and are no longer meant to be.

Tears have value and various qualities. Terms like *bittersweet* and *mixed emotions* refer to this. A variety of emotions can coexist with your steady, fierce joy. Make room for a variety of tears: angry, healing, joy, gratitude, and cleansing tears. As you make room for the tears to flow, you are simultaneously making room for an increased capacity of soul richness and tenderness and widening the inner access trail to your Joy Source. Just as it is customary to have a celebration of life for the passing of a loved one, it's a beautiful symbolic ritual to bless and release the former you and to embrace the new you that you are becoming.

For these circumstances, the masters taught me to tell myself, "That was a step. I'm done with that now."

You have the resources at hand, the Ancient Secrets, to put an end to approval-seeking and to confidently move to your next step. The pleasures of conscious breathing and the rewarding treasures of self-awareness will become far more alluring than stagnant habits.

From the foundation of the Ancient Secrets, we can now begin exploring the fun nuances of self-mastery, to play with as needed, for fully embodying joy and feasting at the buffet of life!

Fierce Joy Action
Menu Secret #3

- Do daily energy cleansing to maintain the flow of life's countless gifts.
- Take time to practice increasing your capacity to focus.
- Enjoy programming your body computer with the portable Quiver of Life stretch.
- Consciously bless and release the former you and embrace who you are becoming today.
- Acknowledge, identify, and nonjudgmentally feel all your emotions.
- Enjoy moving, dancing, exercising, and breathing your affirmations into your body computer.
- Learn the beautiful lessons, upgrade your self-care, and boldly move forward.
- Nurture and enjoy true friendships, the greatest external treasures.
- Explore and nurture your persistent soulful visions.

Daily Joy Reflection

Who or what can I do beautifully without?

CHAPTER 5

Connoisseur of Life
Quality of Breath Equals Quality of Life

While speaking on the phone to a hospitalized friend, who was feeling fear and anxiety, I encouraged him to follow my counts with a few cycles of the Transition Breath. Right before his very eyes, he was amazed at the immediate visible results on his hospital monitor. His blood pressure balanced with just one cycle of guided breathing. He expressed a sighing breath of relief and joy!

We can give ourselves relief from stress and embody joy every day, just as my friend did while lying in a hospital bed anxiously awaiting a diagnosis.

You are now prepared to journey to your inner atmosphere with pleasure. Begin exploring, delighting in the various textures, nuances, vibrations, insights, sensations, light, awareness, and understanding that await your discovery. With the Secrets, you are becoming a connoisseur of breathing awareness, embodying the space within your skin, and curating an inner atmosphere of ever increasing pleasure and ease.

You'll train your mind to follow the streams of breath, peacefully lingering in the stillness of the pauses while allowing your shoulders to melt down away from your ears. Begin engaging your auditory senses and listening to the sound of your breathing, enjoying the kinesthetic feel of the coolness on the way in, the warmth of the exhale after being warmed in your lungs. While you are mentally following the undulating wave, the rise and fall in your body, the breath will become your greatest portable pleasure. You will become masterful in linking your body's signals and sensations with your breathing. Exploring the quality and texture of your breathing will become an adventure in maximizing deeper presence, calmness, and physical ease. You might experience spontaneous healing laughter or tears. Give yourself permission to be surprised by what's revealed.

Mastering your breathing awareness with pranayama is the beginning of mastering yourself. We can be informed of our emotional state by observing the quality of our breathing. Once informed, we can manage and master our emotional state with conscious breathing, penetrating through fear to calmness. We are relaying a message of peace to our nerves, and with a calm, clear mind, we can make wise choices. Also, observing how others are breathing reveals much about their level of calmness or restlessness, which is helpful in understanding. These are all results of being a practicing master of the Secrets and maintaining your fierce joy!

Reactive Breathing – Trauma Breathing

There's a common unhealthy breathing habit in this world, which is a global addiction. We gasp. The gasping habit is not always caused by fear and intimidation. Gasping is often associated with attitudes of superiority. We gossip about what others are doing and gasp, "Look at what they're doing. If they would only do what I think they should do, believe as I believe." We become biochemically addicted to watching the incessantly horrible news and gasp, "How could they do that?" We compete on the highway, and when we abruptly get cut off in traffic, we gasp.

A gasping breath is a mini trauma to our bodies. It fires up the sympathetic nervous system, our fight-or-flight response, which evolved from back when we had to duck and dodge dinosaurs. This response is an important instinct under dangerous circumstances, but habits of reacting to all the bad news, clickbait, gossiping, and road raging create a chronic state of unhealthy fight or flight. Each gasp signals danger to the nerves. That's a high price to pay for engaging in petty gossip, which, by the way, is another form of approval-seeking to feel a sense of belonging.

The connection to joy is diminished when the vitality of life is invested in petty gossip, squabbling, aggressive driving, or wallowing in bad news. Many of the preventable attitudes that lead to a gasping breath create a biochemical reaction. This results in an unhealthy form of excitement that begins to feel normal. Without a focused creative outlet, it's easy to confuse the adrenal rush of gasping with living fully.

To restore a feeling of calmness and ease within your skin, treat yourself to a long, soft exhale while dropping your shoulders and relaxing your belly. Long- and soft-sighing exhales send a reassuring message of calmness to your nerves. The message is then relayed from your nerves to calm your mind, calm your body, and calm your emotions. Needless gasping is a detrimental thing to do to yourself. Forgive yourself for gasping and restore yourself with calming breaths.

Baseline of Calm, Steady Joy

Recalling my twenties, how I used to pack in the maximum amount of fun social events and activities: One day, I'd feel full of vigor, vim, vitality, and pep, then the next day, I find myself puzzled as to why I felt wiped out. Sometimes, I would even fall ill. I searched for solutions for maintaining nonstop exuberance, wrongfully thinking that it was natural. In my youthful folly, I thought only old people needed quiet, restful time. I assumed I needed to ingest something, like more vitamins, tofu, the latest protein powder, or to do an external activity, like increasing exercise. Nothing I did or ate provided the unrealistic results I was looking for. I was not suffering from a tofu deficiency!

Eventually, I stumbled upon the science of psychoneuroimmunology. PNI explained the cause of my extreme high- and low-energy swings. Too much chronic excitement taxes the nerves, resulting in lowered immunity and vulnerability to microbes and germies that pervade our world.

Overexuberance, a form of unrestrained excitement, dissipates focus and vital energy. In my twenties, I got a speeding ticket. At the traffic school I attended, the teacher referred to youth who speed as "exuberant drivers." I was guilty as charged. From the science of PNI, I now know that being in a rush is a rush to the grave. The Ancient Secrets have led me to value life balance and the embodied state of steady joy far more than the highs and lows of external stimulation. This has resulted in my own steady health. With nonexuberant driving, I've also come to value lower auto insurance rates.

Calmness is a precursor to focus and concentration. When you're calm, you don't make mistakes. The Secrets transform overwhelm into balance and calm efficiency. Calmness is an embodied state of being that can be cultivated, and with regular practice, calmness will become your baseline. If a worry suddenly overtakes you or you are exposed to someone's contagious mood of anger or anxiety, you will immediately sense the disruption of your peace, a wobble in your baseline of calm, steady joy. If the cause of the disruption is not addressed, calm efficiency flies out the window, and chaos ensues. Having developed a strong, steady baseline of calmness, I now immediately identify every wobble and ask myself, "What, or who, just happened that disrupted my baseline?" I waste no time. I immediately get to the bottom of it and apply the Secrets to reestablish my connection to fierce joy. Incessant excitement leaks power, wreaking havoc on health. Connecting with the infinite wellspring of joy within renews and replenishes vitality and is superior to any external thrill!

Double-Duty Discipline

This is the downside of self-mastery and why it feels lonely at the top. Expressing fierce joy is rare because it keeps you out of the anxiety-ridden fray of mass consciousness. It's human nature to wobble emotionally. Unchecked emotional instability causes misery and suffering, and misery loves company. The desire to belong is so strong in dense human conditioning that people will bond in misery. Misery clubs have a need to blame and vilify others, thereby feeling justified in hostile behavior. They are dangerous. Miserable people will do everything they can to dampen joy. Miserable people despise and are jealous of joy. When you're focused, disciplined, and doing what it takes to fulfill the joy found with the Secrets, it's necessary to be aware of those who would be happy to rob your joy. Remember and affirm, "I am not responsible for anybody's moods."

This is the double duty that is required for maintaining your fierce joy. Miserable people are lazy about identifying and managing their own moods. They will argue for their limitations and misery. Consider the old man on the porch; he'd rather whine to a five-year-old and cast blame all day long than be accountable for his life choices. The company of joy that is found in the Secrets is far superior to becoming a member of a misery club. When you remain connected to the purity of your fierce joy, you belong to the eternal joy club. This is not to feel superior, but rather, to fully enjoy life. You can be the connoisseur at the buffet of life, choosing the variety of treats from your fierce joy action menus. You can be the embodiment of fierce joy.

Expansion of your spirit will stir up fears in others, especially if they're used to you playing the role of the doormat in their life. Joy robbers love the role of feeling superior. When you've put yourself in their energy's clutches, they can sense your flourishing expansion. You're no longer available for them to step on, which will feel like a threat to their petty identity.

I've experienced this at every level of moving onto new horizons. When I see that my students and clients have achieved the golden glow of serenity—of self-mastery—I alert them to the double duty that will now be necessary in the company of others. I know that others around them will also sense it. This serenity is visible on their face and in their demeanor. This is a result of the comfort and trust they've developed with their reliable Joy Source. Some respond to this calmness with admiration, others with hostility.

Joy disturbs those with unaddressed inner demons. These patterns run deep. If you suddenly stop being a doormat, the joy robber will be left with their own uncomfortable feelings of mediocrity.

They sadly and predictably act out jealously with the other's expansion. They will sabotage, manipulate, and try every angle to keep you down. For those who have been conditioned to seek approval, this may sound harsh, but it is the reality of mankind's loony-bin creation. Joy robbers are not aware of or are too lazy to develop the connection to their own Joy Source within. This is not a judgment; this is discernment. Double duty is required every time we're on the highway. It's naïve, foolish, and dangerous to believe other drivers have your best interest and safety at heart.

You may set out at a relaxed pace, enjoying the drive; meanwhile, those who are filled with stress view everyone on the highway as competition, as an impediment to their destination. To maintain your peace on the highway, it is necessary to be aware of the bullies barreling down behind you. With double-duty awareness, you can maintain your safety while calmly maneuvering to allow them to pass you.

Sensing another's stress, you can feel compassion for them while feeling grateful that you are connected to your Joy Source. You are not responsible for the other drivers, but you are responsible for your safety and well-being around other drivers.

The deeper your Joy Source connection, the clearer you will be about the quality of experiences you prefer. When you encounter any kind of pushy person, greedy, controlling, or fast-talking con, you will be ready to say,

"No, thank you." You will get better at it with practice. It's quite freeing to simply say no without explanation.

Quality of life improves when you accept that while doing all you can to maintain fierce joy, not everybody else is. Enjoy the passing pleasures and beauty of life on earth while making the connection to your eternal Joy Source primary. Deepen your connection to Joy Source so securely that you bring it! Bring the joy with you!

As always, let your intuition guide all your relationships and interactions. Every situation is a case-by-case scenario. Fierce joy will lead you to a calm knowing that does not result in reactive flying off the handle. Your intuition may express as a calmly fierce tone of voice, calling out the facts. Righteous anger is a natural, healthy response to being violated. As you use social challenges to become stronger, you will enjoy being supremely comfortable in your own skin. The combination of purity of heart, facts, and calm knowing is great fuel for being authentically, unapologetically you. A like-it-or-lump-it sense of boldness!

Increase Your Tenderness Capacity

With the amount of work it takes to perform the double duty of remembering that you come from joy, while monitoring BFEs, it's important to give yourself respites from the clamor of the world. Spend time in quiet solitude—in cozy, gentle, beautiful environments. Be with those who express gentleness to you. Be gentle with yourself, tenderly pampering yourself and feeling your feelings. Give yourself grace. Spend designated time with the Ancient Secrets.

Life requires that we make one adjustment after another. The fragility of life is always glaringly evident in our faces. Being attached to the way things were, or to particular outcomes, just increases feelings of anxiety, despair, and disappointment. The truth is, life has *always* consisted of changes in personal and world structures, so it behooves you to accept and get used to it. There have been pandemics, wars, economic depressions, social strife, enslavement, corruption, suppression, oppression— *forever*. It's part of mankind's predictable loony-bin creation. Let this inspire you to make your connection to Joy Source creation primary.

Prioritizing time with the Ancient Secrets—being calm, clearheaded, and having my wits about me—gets me through every challenge, and with flying colors. But, like everyone, sometimes I get weary from the adventure of maintaining my wits, and for life balance, I just need to *be*. I need to rest in the pure state of simply being. In the simply being, I savor and enjoy where I am. Who I am becoming has space to emerge. The pause of stillness between the inhale and exhale is a supreme moment to submerge into your inner atmosphere and restore yourself to simply being.

It's ironic that I used to pay for silent retreats. Traditionally, I spent a week in silence from December 23rd to January 2nd to be away from the holiday hustle-bustle, along with intermittent silent retreat weekends throughout the year.

The quality of tenderness would emerge in the consecutive days of silence, tenderness toward myself and others. Tenderness and fierce joy can coexist, and it feels so good to embody both. My home is my silent retreat. Even amidst city noises, the beauty within my Soul Wall saturates the walls of my sanctuary home structure. The two-year-old me who sat among angels, celestial beings, and masters at the Santuario Chimayo pilgrimage was so touched by that experience that I enthusiastically invest my energy in recreating sanctuary wherever I live.

While we're on the topic of quality of life, let me appeal to your vanity and your longevity. Engendering tenderness and appreciation activates growth hormones, which are also considered antiaging. I want to live a long, joyful life, as I decided to do when I encountered the old man sitting on the porch full of blame and regret.

Know that you can increase your capacity to feel tenderness and appreciation. Your body will thank you for it. While it's necessary to set boundaries to block violating joy robbers, there's no limit to the amount of tenderness you can safely feel within your Soul Wall.

Playful and Sarcastic

Mom and Dad expressed fun, playful, harmless humor. Their playful style is reminiscent of the late Victor Borg, a comedian, conductor, and pianist. I found his performances to be consistently hilarious and wholeheartedly agree with his saying, "Laughter is the shortest distance between two people."

My maternal grandmother and a couple of others weaponized humor with treacherous sarcasm, hurling soul-crushing psychic darts at others while half laughing and half sneering. Growing up, I got firsthand experience with the results of both styles of humor. Around the sarcastic relatives, I recall feeling a density, a weight in the atmosphere around them. In my effort to understand the drain I felt from the barbs they routinely dished out at family gatherings, I discovered the origins of the word sarcasm. It comes from Greek, meaning "to tear flesh." That's how it felt, like my soul was being swiped at, shredded. I witnessed the facial expressions of sinking pain on others who were victimized by cleverly crafted emotional gut punches. As a stand-up comedian, I've consciously chosen to follow my parents' example. Mankind's world offers plenty of material to create comic relief without resorting to cutting sarcasm.

Between some of the fun things we traditionally did—feast, sing, dance, and laugh—talking about other people's business and gossip was included. I'm embarrassed to say that I was guilty of participating. It was part of the unspoken agreement for belonging to the family tribe. By regularly connecting with the beauty of Joy Source, I realized how much this habit of digging up dirt about others was polluting my inner atmosphere. I also became aware of how others get stuck in the habit of being overly invested in my personal business. It's human nature.

These unseen negative energy projections create detrimental joy leaks. When I sense another's limited BFE being projected to me, I expand my Soul Wall of fierce joy to block them out. In order to maintain the beauty of my inner atmosphere, I also need to leave everybody else alone in my mind. Their business is their business. I'm the final authority on me, relying on my intuition, the faculty of my soul. I'm free. You're free. Everyone else is free. In my mind, we're all free.

This used to be a necessary and daily reminder to myself to leave others alone in my mind. Not anymore; I've trained myself to mind my own business mentally. It's now a pleasure to reclaim that surplus of bandwidth for fun and self-care. To reinforce this habit, I affirm, "I'm a full-time job." Fierce joy is also required to manage the jobs of double duty and being aware of others' intentions, which is a lot of work. This work is well worth it because it results in continuity of vitality, health, and fun.

During my years of teaching yoga and meditation, I developed the skill of identifying the student's depth of connection to their inner atmosphere by the movement or stillness under their closed eyelids. Fidgety eyeballs reveal a fidgety, restless mind. At the beginning of class, almost all had furrowed brows and fluttery eyelid movements. I'd jokingly remind them at every class, while guiding them to turn inward, "Now leave everyone else alone in your mind. Mind your own business." And, without fail there would be giggles of guilt, every class. This moment of comic relief through self-awareness brought the students' minds into the moment. Freeing others from their minds for a bit allowed them to more fully embody the space within their skins. Coming to my class was their designated time to do this. As soon as I saw the fidgety eyeballs return, I'd repeatedly remind them, "Get back here. You can return to other people's business after class if you'd like. This is your time to take care of yourself."

We love to ruminate and talk about what other people are doing, mostly faultfinding. This is a huge part of social media culture and the terrible daily news. Focusing outward is human nature; gossip is rampant and insidious. Being up in arms, criticizing, and condemning is a global pastime. While I am aware of important social issues, I am here to enjoy a life of meaning and fun with a tender heart. With this perspective, I am able to contribute helpful service to others from a feeling of surplus rather than pointless complaining.

With the passage of time, I'm finally able to acknowledge and appreciate two gifts that my miserable grandmother gave me. She was a professional dancer, and she saw to it that we got dance lessons. She exemplified the love of movement and body awareness. The second gift was diaries, little blank books for journaling. As an adult, she began giving me hardcover books with blank pages for writing my feelings and dreams. The habit of writing developed my emotional awareness. For these gifts I am eternally grateful. A third "gift" she gave me was an inadvertent cautionary tale, a clear example of how I did not want to be. My parents' playful humor was in stark contrast to my grandmother's. She loved to laugh and had a brilliant, sharp wit mostly fueled by her bitter and scornful nature.

My loving nonbiological grandmother, Ann, helped restore me to wholeness with her kindness and caring words, which carried a palpable vibration filled with prana, the pure substance of life. Dear Ann patched me up in the places that my biological joy-robbing grandmother had shredded.

Laughter at the Buffet of Life

With the broadened perspective of the Secrets, you will begin to laugh more. As you begin standing more firmly on the solid ground of fierce joy, the awareness of human nature's foibles, including your own, will begin to look increasingly absurd. The predictability, ironies, paradoxes, and hypocrisies of mankind's loony-bin world will all come to light, normalized but not numbing. You'll find yourself freaking out less. History makes it evident that masses of people have been acting out in petty and heinous ways forever. The repetitious behavior doesn't make it right, but it's clearly nothing to be surprised about.

It's like the movies we go to see, in genres from comedy to drama and even sci-fi, where tropes, or human patterns, are depicted and played out. We purchase tickets, get our popcorn buttered, and settle in to be entertained with stories of mankind's loony-bin world. We expect that. We pay for that. Mankind's loony-bin behavior continues outside the theater, too, yet we continue to gasp in surprise.

As you begin to recognize the two creations, Joy Source within you and mankind's creation outside of you, you'll easily distinguish which creation you are dwelling in— and dwelling on. You will develop discernment about the quality of emotions you invest in while increasingly embodying your natural state of joy.

Sarcasm is a killjoy, while playful humor restores joy. These are treasures found in my archaeological dig, where I unearthed buried pain, followed by buckets of releasing, cleansing, healing tears. I let the grieving have its way with me until the spectrum swung to laughter, with fierce joy right in the center, my center, my spine, and my brain. This is the freedom that the Ancient Secrets of the masters have led me to. I wish for you this freedom. Know that your archaeological digs will also reveal great treasures of self-awareness that will set you free.

I find it amazing that, physiologically, the "runner's high" results from the increased pumping of the diaphragm, just as the pumping diaphragm in laughter activates joy endorphins. People exercise not only to stay fit but also to let off steam and emotional tension. When we feel overly stressed, the adrenals next to the diaphragm flood our bodies with excessive amounts of the stress hormone cortisol. This can result in a variety of health conditions too long to list here. Laughter gives both stress relief *and* comic relief.

Do your best. Find the absurdities and laugh it off. My friend in the hospital was a real trooper. He began to recognize many of the absurdities within the bureaucracies of the medical system. He found the humor, we laughed, and he breathed consciously, working through many of his fears. This gave him the confidence and clarity of mind to be a strong self-advocate and firmly state his decisions about his medical care.

From your broadened perspective—of humor, calmness, and clarity of mind—you will be able to see, accept, and enjoy the countless gifts of life. By living connected to your Joy Source, you will begin to know what life is opening to you now, today. You will feel it. You will get the message somehow, and it will be different from what your cogitating ego mind suggests. You will see how the information from your Joy Source begins to match with coincidental experiences in the outer creation. Ancient masters teach that there are no coincidences.

The famous Swiss psychologist Carl Jung coined the term *synchronicity* to explain these supernatural experiences, which can seem so wildly freaky and magical. These experiences are related by meaningfulness rather than by cause and effect. In my experience, synchronicities are not random but comforting signs affirming my alignment with the divine. With your calmness, tenderness, and fierce joy under your belt, the adventure of life begins to kick into high gear. Get used to expecting, accepting, and enjoying the synchronicities leading you to the countless gifts of life. When you live from Joy Source, the synchronicities are so natural that they are *supernatural*.

Daily Joy Reflection

How much tenderness can I stand?

CHAPTER 6

Synchronicities
Vision Unfoldment

It was shocking when the fire in my heart went out. After ten solid years of simultaneously training in acting, singing, dancing, and performing in film, theater, and bands, my great love for the stage dwindled. Disappeared. I received very clear signs and encountered extreme obstacles indicating that this was no longer the right direction for me. I felt lost. This was the only time in my life that I felt angry at God, like God had pulled the rug out from under my feet.

During those years, my passionate fire for the performing arts burned for expression, and synchronicities lined up entertainment opportunities. I was interviewed and accepted into the Lee Strasberg Theatre Institute by Anna, Lee's wife. When I came to a financial crunch, my singing teacher there believed in me so much that she granted me a scholarship for another full year. Then the owner of the retail leotard shop I worked at part time gave me a membership to one of the best dance studios in Los Angeles. I took full advantage of that gift, enjoying three to six classes a week. I became an assistant teacher to my favorite teacher. She got me a small role on the hit television series *Family Ties* for dance scenes.

The universe conspired to provide me with dance training, acting school, and the best opera, musical theater, and rock voice teachers. I had cute, playful parents who exemplified a love for people, a good work ethic, and strong spiritual devotion, yet we lived frugally. They were very young when they married. Mom had me when she was only sixteen years old. For this reason, I was grateful for the abundance of opportunities to train and perform with the best.

I thought I was set for life with the role of entertainer, so what happened? Where did the fire go?

I spent a year struggling in deep contemplation, questioning, and finally throwing my hands up in the air. I surrender. What am I supposed to do now? Little did I know that this process of asking, listening, and surrendering would become my daily way of life.

My questions were answered with synchronicities pointing to a fresh start in a new direction. Initially, having a strong ego attachment to the old way of being, I was very resistant. I stubbornly questioned the signs and the visions until a friend who recognized my great passion for the science of meditation hounded me, "You should be teaching yoga!" At the time, I was still struggling to release the attachment to my actress identity while thinking, "Teach yoga? That's ridiculous. Who's going to pay me to teach people how to breathe and roll around on the floor?" Plus, I wasn't sure how to reconcile sharing the metaphysical aspects with the mainstream. But I was desperate; I had nothing to lose. What else could I do?

So, partially to get this friend off my back and at least look into it, I got my teacher certification. Because I had been studying and practicing meditation since the age of fourteen, it turned out that I had a thing or two to teach my teacher. With this realization, I confidently embarked on my new career path. I printed up business cards and was immediately hired to teach. The doors flung open—as they do when you're in alignment. After my temporary identity crisis, I learned to ask, seek, and surrender to guidance by trusting and following instructions. I've learned that things work out well that way, with a harmonious, peaceful flow.

I'd heard about the Native American ritual of doing vision quests. Without much research, I just took the term literally and quested for a vision. After finally maturing out of my resistance to life's flow, I approached the vision quest with openness, ready to receive. I did so with the intention of moving forward with grace rather than clinging to a stagnant role in life. I took myself on a weeklong vacation to reflect in nature. In stillness, I asked, "What's life opening to me now?"

During and after returning from my vision quest getaway, I received visions of doing a yoga video. Again, I threw my hands up in the air, asking, "What are you nuts, God?" I used to say that a lot. Now I say, "Let's go!"

The vision persisted, and the external world fed the inner vision. Synchronicities began rolling in. At that time, people were frequently coming from out of the blue saying, "You should do a yoga video." These were full-blown undeniable messages from both my inner atmosphere and the outer world.

As an act of surrender, on November 1, 1993, I wrote this prayer/affirmation and read it every day:

> Infinite free-flowing Creator, I know you're permeating every aspect of this world, this life, my life. Your gracious and beautiful vision prevails no matter what any person says or thinks. I am one with you and your vision of me and my projects. Your vision is my inspiration. I am fully opening now to more clearly see and express your vision. I am ready and willing now to express your vision. I am knowing that the Perfect Postures for the yoga video are evident. I am certain of your vision of the sequence of yoga postures for this video, and I am certain that these postures and the loving consciousness of this video will uplift, inspire, and increase the feeling of well-being to all who view it. I am knowing and clear about my choices. For this gift and all God's gifts I am grateful. I open my heart wide with love and appreciation to God and for God's guidance. Thank you, God. Thank you. It is already done now. It is fully accomplished. God's vision is here now. So be it. Amen.

On February 25, 1994, approximately three months after I wrote the vision prayer/affirmation, I received a call from a club manager where I taught yoga. She announced that talent scouts from Paramount Studios wanted to meet me about creating a yoga video for the *Buns of Steel* fitness label and to be part of their new mind-body series. The "buns" and my quickly growing classes qualified me. So, there I was back in Hollywood, entertaining, but in a new way. I wrote a script, which the producer and film crew used as a guide on the film location. The script flowed through me while in a meditative state, and much of the video's introduction includes words from my prayer/affirmation. Surprisingly, the producer wholeheartedly approved of the words. I received half of my advance on March 15, 1994, and the balance on April 5, 1994. The video was released shortly after that.

This all unfolded within five months of surrendering to the vision. While this may appear to be a quick turnaround time, I discovered that after crossing the threshold into any new vision, focus and discipline are required to maintain continuity of forward motion. It's not a time to rest on your laurels.

Living by one's inner vision is always fulfilling, yet becoming comfortable with the unknown is an acquired taste. It takes some getting used to. The grumpy old man on the porch, full of blame and regret, inadvertently showed me the outcome of not listening to Joy Source. By complaining and remaining in his sad, worn out, *known* victim story, joy eluded him. The *unknown* has become a lifestyle for me. There's nothing stagnant about it. It's always fresh. I use the Secrets to penetrate into stillness, asking, listening, observing synchronicities, and following instructions. What is *known* in this lifestyle is that I can trust my Joy Source to reveal the way to goodness for myself and all who are involved.

The above example of an internationally distributed video is bigger and flashier than my daily synchronicities, but they are all of equal value to me. I walk with the guidance leading in everything I do, even grocery shopping, for every basic need. This trust engenders the continuity of ease within my skin. Synchronicities are all puzzle pieces to an ever-unfolding picture, a vision that goes beyond the intellect and the ego.

Reflecting back on my life, it is absolutely clear that I have been guided every step of the way. My intuition, visions, literal signs on billboards and bumper stickers, collaborative people, perfect song lyrics popping into my mind, particular birds making their presence known, and opportunities coming "from outta the blue" all reassure me of that consistent guidance. Did I always honor these benevolent guideposts? No. I did like we all do at times: doubted myself, fearfully clinging to the comfortable but stagnant known. Part of me also feared the inevitable scorn and jealousy that comes from others when they sense someone is reaching for broader horizons. Plus, I sometimes took to heart others' limited opinions and allowed them to sway me.

There's no shortage of people who like to plant seeds of doubt about what we know is true for ourselves. Being true to yourself, to your innate vision, is the most challenging yet rewarding thing anyone can do. Be yourself in the world, not of it.

There were many times that my stubborn ego wanted to hang onto some obsolete role in life, a fantasy, and to control the outcome. Letting the ego's desires win out over the guidance of my Joy Source has always led to stagnation, a fruitless dead end. Listening to, surrendering to, and trusting what comes from Joy Source always results in having my needs met, and then some. Daily discipline is required to weed through the incessant bombardment of external BFEs and to maintain focus on Joy Source. The Secrets will help you penetrate the restless noise of mankind's creation and listen in stillness. It takes courage to completely trust. The test of time will prove the trustworthiness of your vision's synchronicities. After you develop that trust, you'll see that synchronicities are the trusted trail to the vision.

Vision Quest Ritual Tips

If you notice, the word question has the word quest within it. You've got to ask questions to get answers. Beware of the ego or conditioning of old fears that may have you holding onto a desired answer while you're questing. It doesn't work like that. This will result in spinning confusion. In fact, this approach is at cross purposes with receiving because you are outwardly projecting a BFE.

Vision-questing is an inner request to your Joy Source, requiring you to be open and receptive.

This is the time to fervently implement the Secrets in order to calm your nerves, come into stillness, and access the purity of your baby spine and brain. We then become that open channel for Joy Source to lead the way. Give yourself grace as you move into the freshness of the unknown, as you would with an innocent baby. Be prepared to take incremental steps forward, like the baby's cycle of developing strength to roll over, crawl, stand, and eventually run.

In my experience, the visions don't immediately make logical sense. Here are some clues to look for. Your heart is just drawing you to do something; go someplace or research a new direction you suddenly feel curious about. If you prefer strawberry flavor over chocolate, you don't need a logical explanation if that is what is most satisfying. The vision also defies explanation and feels like being struck by Cupid's arrow. The longer the vision churns, the more the heart and soul experience a deepening, rich soul cry of yearning to follow through. Then, the synchronicities that match the internal vision begin to appear.

I always use reason to follow up responsibly in taking action toward the vision. I move as I'm led to, step by step. Initially, visions just don't make logical sense. They feel like purely unknown adventures, but when I get there, the synchronicities—peaceful, fun-flowing, and inspiring social interactions—reassure me that I am in the right place at the right time.

Then "What are you nuts, God?" becomes "Oh, this is why I was drawn here." Joy! Receiving a vision is always different than what you're currently doing. For this reason, it will likely feel daunting until you get into the swing of listening. If this is the case, I suggest you continue inquiring about the vision. Keep asking for as many signs as you need. Joy Source is inexhaustible.

A few years ago, I was led to make a change that was such a beautiful new level of abundance and prosperity that I had a hard time wrapping my brain around it. I couldn't believe it. I hounded my Joy Source for signs. And I got them, repeatedly, with variations on the signs. They all repeatedly pointed in the same direction. I felt like a little girl who'd been given an oversized queen's robe and a crown too big for my head. But I used my reasoning, and it was easily possible for me to take the plunge responsibly. It took me two months to psychologically grow into the robe and crown. I cried joy tears while saying, "Really, God, I get to have all this?"

Even success requires adapting and a change in one's mindset. Now, I'm saying, "Thank you, God. I've adapted. What else do You have up Your sleeve? Let's go!" As my abundance increases, I'm eagerly looking forward to contributing more to causes that have meaning to me and greatly benefit others. This is not to appear virtuous. In a way, it's a selfish motive. Doing this gives me a rich soul feeling, like a warm glowing smile within my skin. And after overgiving to draining joy robbers for so long, it's a pleasurable switch to give where it makes a meaningful difference and increases my joy, all at once.

Vision-questing has led me to fun new paths, like becoming a comedian, and some that are just plain old practical, but all are satisfying. For instance, during the pandemic lockdown, I vision-quested and was given a trail of synchronicities that led to organically forming a yoga class in the park. I began to synchronistically bump into former students (some called, emailed, and messaged). I'd been doing my own meditations out in the park anyway. We were all so grateful to have some structure during that strange time of blurry schedules. Our weekly classes gave us a reason to get outdoors in the sunshine and fresh air and move while sharing support and friendship. I didn't logically plan it. I'd quested and followed the synchronicities, and the vision unfolded. Together, we pleasurably got through the pandemic, one of the darkest times in global history.

Affirmative Objects and Actions

Every cell of your body is a hologram of the universe. What you think, say, feel, and do sends a message to your universe(s). These messages are seeds that potentially bloom. For this reason, I find it fun, simple, and easy to support my inner vision with external objects and by taking vision-related actions. Objects in your environment have associations that engender certain feelings that communicate to your universe. Actions reinforce feelings in your body.

First, I recommend discarding objects that have a negative association. Consciously release and bless the memories and people involved while integrating the lesson associated with the object. Anchor in the new direction of your vision by giving thanks for the beautiful lesson. Some stuff may not have a negative association but have become irrelevant to your current lifestyle and unfolding vision. These are external distractions that leak joy. For instance, documents, files, and even uniforms from a former business can be thrown out. These actions relay the message to your universe (cells) that you're cleaning the slate of your *outer* environment to make room for the new systems that support your vision. The Secrets clear the slate of your *inner* atmosphere for receiving your highest vision.

After discarding obsolete objects, you can purchase delightful affirmative objects as vision reminders. For instance, long ago when I had a roommate, that person had a rickety vacuum cleaner that seemed to be held together by paper clips and electrical tape. To prepare for having my own place, I sent a message to my universe by investing in a deluxe vacuum cleaner. Once I got my own place, that vacuum cleaner continued to serve as a reminder. Affirmative objects are a treat to give to your universe, filling your cells with joyful anticipation. Affirmative objects are a way to enjoy the pre-celebration of the manifested vision. These support you in joyfully looking forward to life's upcoming gifts.

As an example, perhaps you dream of traveling. An affirmative object could be getting the perfect luggage. Another affirmative action would be getting your passport. As your vision unfolds, you're ready to flow into it. Have fun, and use your imagination with affirmative objects while being responsible and within your financial means. Watch the synchronicities line up, like countless gifts of life.

Visualization – Transmitted BFEs

There's a formula to play with for revealing joy from the inside out. After receiving the incessant vision from Joy Source to produce a yoga video, followed by synchronicities from the external world, I did affirmative actions by putting pictures of exercise videos from a Target ad onto a dream board. This visual aid became an affirmative object. I also read my video prayer/affirmation every day, speaking the vision into my universe. All of the above supports you in coming into the feeling state of already having the fulfilled vision. The next step is to express deep gratitude along with the embodied feeling of already having it. You are programming your magnificent body computer for vision fulfillment.

Keep in mind that *vision* comes before *visualization*. It's ideal to visualize the vision (that you know within your heart and soul) aligned with the purity of your Joy Source. You may manifest a desire by visualizing without the purity of Joy Source, but this usually has repercussions. Visualizing your vision brings with it the flow of beautiful, amazing synchronicities. Vision from Joy Source is imbued with eternal goodness. It's ideal to set forth your vision into motion from this purity of intention.

Affirmation Creation

Early on, prior to my archeological digs of self-inquiry, many of my unconscious affirmations were formed by what I wanted to get away from. And I got exactly that: people and situations to get *away from*. When I changed the focus of my affirmations to what I wanted to *move toward*, life began moving me forward into more peaceful, flowing, loving experiences. That simple awareness of language intention created a world of difference for me. I was in such awe of the beautiful harmony, creative fulfillment, and increased prosperity that it actually took me a couple of months to adjust to so much good. I'm used to it now. The Ancient Secrets work!

The human body is the most magnificent computer in the universe. What you say to yourself is what you are doing to yourself. Your cells are like emojis expressing whatever you tell yourself. You get to be in charge of the programming, going beyond limited opinions, your own or from others. You get to choose your thoughts and attitudes. This does not mean that emotions are overridden with denial or stuffed down. The full spectrum of emotions must be identified, acknowledged, and expressed in a harmless manner to self and others in order to maintain your joy connection.

No matter how many pretty words you cleverly string together, denied emotions will leak out unconsciously and sometimes with severe consequences. When a joy robber attacks with diminishing, discounting, or discrediting words, you can use your feelings of frustration, hurt, and anger to fuel your affirmative words effectively. Others' put-downs are an opportunity to step up into your truth while using others' negativity as sod under your feet to stand on. Consider the limiting words that are projected onto you. Then, choose countering words that affirm the opposite. Fuel these affirmative words with the fierce conviction of your emotions out loud or in writing. Joy Source's vision of you is the ultimate vision.

Whether you think, write, or speak your words, strong emotions provide the powerful substance of conviction you need for embodying your affirmations. A surefire way to embody and assimilate your affirmation is to enjoy moving with your affirmation, exercise it, and dance it deep into your cells. This will move the affirmation from the intellect into your body, transforming approval-seeking into boldness and fun.

Whether you speak your affirmation to yourself, to an external robber, or write it, this will flip the joy robber's projected lower vibes and raise yours! Honor, value, and reroute your emotions to program your magnificent body computer out of the grip of limited projections. Always let your calm, intuitive knowing guide you back to your fierce joy.

Daily Joy Reflection

What's life opening to me now?

Spiral of Eternity

Infinitely long
the spiral going round,
with creative changes
the soul is upward bound.

Winding up the spiral,
man is living evolution,
awareness always growing,
seeking man's solution.

Expansion ever broader,
souls reach for the top,
continually adapting,
the journey will not stop.

Souls moving higher,
wider the spiral becomes,
returning to old lessons,
until the learning is done.

Upward momentum,
the soul who learns fast,
lessons learned well,
soon let go to the past.

Continually reaching,
unconscious of what he's after,
the soul will one day realize,
of his Self he is Master.

By Marguerite Baca

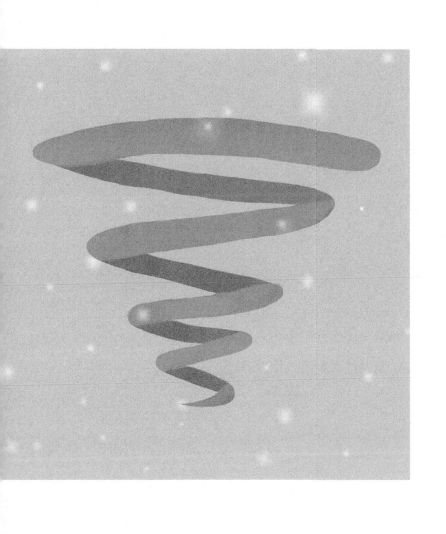

CHAPTER 7

Inventing and Reinventing Yourself

Ever-New Becoming

Identity Crisis

After the fire temporarily went out for the work in acting, the new role of teaching yoga opened up. Once I stopped freaking out and surrendered, I understood the beautiful lesson. It was my attachment to a role in life that caused me emotional pain and suffering: an identity crisis. I learned that the roles I play are what I do, not who I am. I come from joy. I am joy. To joy I will return. My true identity is joy.

I also learned to reject limiting roles that others project onto me. I do not project onto others, but for discernment, I do acknowledge how others act and behave more than what they say. I am free in joy, and I set others free in my mind. I've learned to internally frame the roles I play in life as something I do. For instance, I reframe in my mind, "I am a yoga teacher" to "I teach yoga" and "I'm a comedian" to "I do stand-up comedy." All roles change. Some people identify so strongly with a role that they become violent, depressed, or suicidal when their role changes.

Nonattachment to roles allows me to be fluid with life's unfolding vision while increasing comfort with the unknown. Moving through cycles of life and the various stages requires constantly letting go of obsolete roles. You are also not your stories. With time, stories pile up. Being attached to roles and stories will rob you of today's countless gifts. My true, unchanging self is that pure joy that's been flowing into my brain and spine since conception. Nonattachment to roles assists in remaining free of the ego's defenses and identity crises. Growing pains are inevitable, but so worth the growing. The alternative is stagnation or worse.

Be mindful of any words you think, speak, or write that follow the two words "I am." Ask your Joy Source to guide every word you think, speak, and write. Claim and celebrate the beautiful, empowering lessons learned from your changing roles and stories. Continue to reveal, remember, know, and affirm that "I am joy."

Existential Crisis

The Secrets bring forth the countless gifts of life in continuity, just as the great masters taught me. A few years ago, I began to master this continuity, maintaining consistent calmness of mind, calmness of body, and calmness of emotions. This is the foundation for embodying fierce joy. Surprisingly, the experience of continuity resulted in an existential crisis. While I was enjoying peace, health, and calm efficiency, it became glaringly clear, by contrast, that much of mankind's world is filled with fear, disease, and chaos. Joy robbers abound. This caused me to wonder, "Why am I here?" I quested for the answer to "Why do I exist?"

I began an assessment of my values, and the only thing that makes existing feel worth it to me is *fun*. That's what gives me the most meaning. I have fun employing the Secrets and sharing with all who are receptive. It's fun for me to see others come into the soft golden glow of serenity that results from knowing their Joy Source. Even in the face of challenges, there's a reassurance that comes from my relationship with Joy Source. Overcoming obstacles becomes a fun adventure.

It's fun for me to see others develop the boldness to fulfill their personal vision. It's fun to witness others enjoying the adventure of their synchronicities. The synchronicities provide daily meaningful pleasures and fun solutions. While aiming for a goal, there is no sense of impatience or waiting—because there are pleasures to enjoy today.

To experience continuity of joy requires fluidly reinventing yourself as your roles in life change. To minimize or avoid an identity crisis, always plan something to look forward to. Find daily, simple pleasures to enjoy. If you have a planner, be sure to plan some fun—*your* definition of fun. To make the Secrets a regular part of your daily life, include them in your planner. Give yourself grace if you find yourself slacking. Put a little effort in each day (and the next day) until the effort becomes a natural part of your life that you look forward to. Be diligent in reframing dread into joy so that you express enthusiasm. Have goals beyond your goals. This provides a fail-safe that will keep you focused on your vision unfoldment while leaving distracting BFEs behind to eat your dust.

Defining Meaning and Success

In my twenties, I landed a position at a big-shot advertising agency. I had a great salary and even a company car. I thought I'd hit the big time—until a year later when I looked at my closet stuffed with gorgeous clothes and realized I'd become a compulsive shopper. Every day, I was spending a total of three hours in traffic, going back and forth to work. I had zero passion for the work, and no amount of fancy clothing labels could fill the void. I quit the ad agency job, found part-time work, and explored education and training in the arts, which lit my fire!

One fun and interesting part-time job was as a receptionist for a successful, wealthy, handsome attorney at an entertainment law firm in Los Angeles. I got to meet some amazing, kind, talented celebrities in a beautiful high-rise with spectacular views of the city. Sounds dreamy, doesn't it? In the end, it became a tragic cautionary tale. The lawyer, who was married with a young child, began an affair with a famous, glamorous actress. He delighted in seeing himself in the tabloids with her. As the receptionist, I was caught in the cross fire. The actress would incessantly call and yell, demanding he speak to her now! She made it clear that he was to drop everything and interrupt all his meetings when she called. His abandoned wife, filled with bitterness and sadness, called with the same demanding tone, using the son's needs to leverage guilt. Between the two of them, I sure got an earful.

The lure of rubbing elbows with the rich and famous got the better of the soft-spoken, starstruck lawyer. He left his wife and child, married the actress, and a few years later put a gun to his head and shot himself. Wealth, fame, good looks, and financial success did not provide enough meaning for him to want to live. While gloating over some passing worldly prestige, he completely lost his connection to his Joy Source.

We're all seekers—but searching for what exactly? This is for each individual to explore and discover for themselves. While we may have overlapping shared hobbies or values with others, finding what is most personally meaningful requires regular soul-searching. The external world sends a daily barrage of BFEs in an attempt to sell us on temporary satisfactions, which can lure us away from the purity of Joy Source. With the passage of time and new experiences under our belts, what has meaning and value to us changes, along with our personal definitions of success.

Once you find the fierce, unshakable Joy Source within you and begin to embody joy, the search is over. This experience of joy cannot be topped by anything in mankind's loony-bin creation. This is all a passing show for our education and entertainment, offering us daily lessons for mastering balance and opening us to the countless gifts of life.

It's human nature to assume, to put words in others' mouths, ruminate about how others should do as we think, believe as we believe, and do as we do. There's a tendency to invest more thought into changing others than investing in perfecting our own states of calmness, health, and fun. Focusing on others' business is a form of self-neglect. Self-neglect and low self-esteem are partners.

Tending to your inner atmosphere—the quality of your breathing, the level of your calm efficiency, and your capacity for tenderness—doesn't leave much time for being nosy or pushy. There's a saying that I certainly claim to be true for me, "I am a full-time job." The more I leave others alone, including in my thoughts, the more bandwidth I have for my well-being and responsibilities. This results in calm efficiency, fun, and a tender heart. They are my personal, primary markers of success. I put health at the top of the list, and the qualities of calmness, fun, and tenderness are prerequisites. Without these feelings, all the riches or fancy labels in the world would not mean much to me. Doing your personal best is its own reward. You will sleep well at night by settling all accounts, financial and social, and maintaining a clear conscience.

It's tempting to believe that having a clever mind is superior to tenderness. Mental acuity is of great value for reasoning, yet the cogitating mind can easily override tenderness. Aligning heart and soul is cleverest of all. We are passing through this temporal world. The Joy Source that descended into our embryonic systems is eternal.

After successfully graduating from lessons, you will see everything you've seen before, but with fresh eyes and a new depth of richness, awe, courage, and beauty. Fierce joy, being the protective attribute of your soul, will allow you to maintain your tender heart, free of bitterness. Be free of regret and blame, unlike the old man on the porch. Be free.

Continuity of Joy Action Menu

- Always plan something to look forward to.
- Learn to enjoy learning and become a lifelong learner.
- Include the Ancient Secrets in your planner so they become part of your lifestyle.
- Give yourself grace while developing will power for new habits.
- Put a little effort in each day until new habits become a pleasurable part of your life.
- Diligently reframe dread into joy so that you express enthusiasm in everything you do.
- Have goals beyond your goals and celebrate every milestone.
- Continue evaluating the quality of every BFE that you transmit and receive.
- Feel and express gratitude for your Joy Source.

Daily Joy Reflection

What can I do today that feels meaningful to me?

CHAPTER 8

Have the Last Laugh

The Greatest Treasures of Life

Loony-Bin Creation

The Ancient Secrets will change you. They will lead you to the countless gifts of life and toward safety, provision, and protection. It's not your imagination. Eventually, you will feel surprised at how you don't freak out like you used to over standard adult responsibilities and life's curve balls. Rather than gasping in surprise at every bit of weirdness around you in this temporal world, you'll develop an acceptance that mankind's creation has always been full of predictable loony-bin behaviors.

The external circumstances of the loony-bin creation are always changing, while the joy creation you come from is a steady, stable source. As you solidly anchor here, at the core of your being, common human behaviors in mankind's creation don't surprise or throw you off. You will also freak out less about what others are doing yet joyfully freak out in amazement at the calm, efficient person you've become.

In college, majoring in criminal law, I was required to study cases in the law library filled with volumes of crime stories. I remember shaking my head with the revelation that if there is some bizarre-ass shenanigan or heinous thing to do, somebody has done it or will do it.

We're conditioned in mankind's loony-bin creation with limited loony-bin beliefs. We're all in it, but with the Secrets, it is possible to be in it—but not of it. Loony is a spectrum. We all contain the full spectrum of loony human emotions. It's how we manage these emotions that defines the level of our loony-ness. From the emotion of frustration, one person may act harmfully to self or others, while another might dance it off or rationally file a lawsuit. Calm, clear intuition should lead the way. When you're calm, you don't make mistakes.

During self-inquiry, listening to the voice of life, that pure substance within you, you will begin to sense the quality of vibrations around you more keenly: the good, bad, and the ugly. All of it. You will begin moving through life with a flowing sure-footedness, poise, and impervious joy.

With the self-awareness born of swadhyaya (self-inquiry), you will be aware of being in mankind's loony-bin creation while remaining free of it. You will develop peace beyond understanding. By knowing and being anchored to the state of joy, you will remain free of the ever-changing trance of illusion and the changing circumstances outside of you. Being connected to your joy is the best source of calmness, clarity, solutions, answers, guidance, intuition, inspiration, and vision. Joy Source is your one-stop shop. The Secrets get you there.

Comic Relief – Stress Relief

There's a story behind the comedian stage name I played with for a while. Baby Dolly Lama Baca came to me when I was teaching on campus one day and mobs of people were entering the campus to hear the Dalai Lama speak. Even though I was teaching in a classroom, and he was in an auditorium, in my imagination I playfully thought to myself, the Dalai Lama and I are both presenters today. Yes, I have a fun, vivid imagination. My mom's term of endearment for me was Baby Girl, so that day I deemed myself Baby Dolly Lama Baca. It's fun to say and always gives me a giggle.

An example of an amusing irony in this loony-bin world was that some students were scalping Dalai Lama tickets for hundreds of dollars, while his talk was about integrity and compassion. By observing the ironies, hypocrisies, and paradoxical nature of the world, you become aware of mankind's petty and destructive behaviors. Because these behaviors are historically predictable, the dramas that are playing out can become educational, amusing, and sometimes hilarious. With your surplus of fierce joy, you will be equipped to help those who are receptive. You will be able to uplift those who are suffering. With your abundance of vitality, you can volunteer or donate resources to a cause you care deeply about. Yet, keep in mind, some are not interested in growing. When this is the case, spare your joy energy and move on.

With the self-awareness you attain from the Secrets, you begin to understand yourself and, therefore, human nature. As you observe the theater of your mind, become entertained by your discoveries. Be grateful for discovering your diminishing thoughts and the looping mental conversations in your mind, and laugh at the absurdities you've layered over your pure Joy Source. When you get to this place, you begin to really enjoy being you!

As I began to book regular stand-up gigs, I sensed that the comedian Jerry Seinfeld, the Dalai Lama, and I all had something in common. Clearly all three of us laugh a lot, but we also laugh at mankind's pettiness. The hit show *Seinfeld* was called "the show about nothing." Joy Source is the only something that is steady in our ever-changing circumstances. The characters are all manipulative and petty, expressing common human loony-bin tendencies. Millions find this funny because it's so relatable to how we are conditioned to believe, think, and act. The show's characters are not practicing masters of the Ancient Secrets—quite the opposite.

Recently I discovered another commonality with Jerry Seinfeld. He's been a dedicated meditator for decades. As a comedian, Seinfeld copiously writes about his observations of people and life. I have been doing this same practice since childhood, beginning with keeping diaries. Since performing in stand-up comedy, I now use my observations to glean the absurdities of human nature.

Know that the broadened perspective you glean from the Secrets will likely result in great humor. When I meditate, I often have the funniest thoughts and laugh out loud.

It would almost seem like an interruption, but the joy is actually an enhancement. At these moments, I feel and see the light of my core brighten and expand.

Cussing Blessing

I have a personal secret to share. I do enjoy cuss words. For me, they add balance to our world of duality, especially when it comes to valuing peace while living in a loony-bin world. Cuss words are a healthy coping mechanism for me. My mom loves to remind me how, even as a child, I would chide her when she would complain about somebody. I'd always say, "Oh, Mom, God bless their ass." As an adult, I see the value of acknowledging the existence of joy robbers while minimizing their significance in light of the infinite Joy Source. I release them with my cussing blessing and make myself laugh all at the same time.

Flick the Fleas

One strategy that is especially fun for gaining perspective on petty joy robbers is to do what I call "flick the fleas." I began implementing it with sheer glee and satisfaction when I went through the rough two years of standing up to the corrupt national organization. Being incessantly called into hostile meetings gave me plenty of flea-flicking practice.

When you encounter the common joy robbers who try to establish their superiority by putting you down, you can secretly do a flicking gesture under a desk or table. When a petty joy robber's words or actions echo in your mind when you're alone, you're free to elaborately celebrate flicking the flea. Hold both hands in the air, do the flick gesture, then widely spread your palms while doing a joy dance. This simple physical gesture communicates to your body you do not accept limiting thoughts from yourself or others. Feel the freedom while physically affirming fierce joy. Embody fierce joy!

As you learn to manage your own moods and laugh at your foibles, begin to find your go-to funny responses to situations. This will allow you to consciously transmute the stress hormone cortisol with the healing, comic relief of joy endorphins. Comic relief is stress relief.

Along with "God bless their ass," "eat my dust," and "toodle-oo," I also get a kick out of using the funny line, "kiss my grits," coined by the actress Polly Holliday, who played a sassy waitress on the TV show *Alice*, in the late 1970s. The country song title "Did I Shave My Legs for This?" is a handy response I frequently use to give myself comic relief from disappointing situations. Another lighthearted and true reminder to keep in your back pocket is the quote from George Bernard Shaw, "Never wrestle with a pig. You both get dirty, and the pig likes it." That's Shaw's lighthearted wisdom for the serious-ass issue of joy robbers.

The Greatest Inner Treasure – Self-Awareness

To patch up leaking joy and reclaim it after rolling in pig mud, find the humor, ironies, paradoxes, absurdities, pettiness, and even pain from the circumstances.

Humor slices through the *maya* (Sanskrit for illusion). It cuts through the appearances of ever-changing circumstances, returning you to that which is unchanging, the joy you come from, the joy that is your true nature. In the practice of swadhyaya (self-inquiry), all is included, bringing the opportunity to become educated with life's wisdom and, ideally, entertained by observing the roles we're playing. The roles inevitably change as we move into new stages of life. We can go dragging our feet or move forward, fortified by power. Material things can deteriorate, be stolen, and destroyed, but self-awareness is an eternal treasure we get to keep in the storehouse of our consciousness.

The Greatest Outer Treasure – True Friendship

True friends mutually extend BFEs imbued with the purity of joy, loyalty, goodness, trust, and generosity. The treasure of true friendship brings the priceless gift of an embodied huge, warm inner soul smile. True friendship brings warmth that saturates your entire inner atmosphere and radiates out. A true friend gives genuine support that engenders a deeper embodiment of fierce joy. There's no need to brace yourself as you would around a joy robber. With a sincere soul, your purity of joy feels unfettered, light, and free, so much so that you naturally look forward to seeing them again. You smile at the mere thought of them and feel deep gratitude. Laughter, goose bumps of inspiration, and joy tears are common embodied occurrences between true friends.

Train yourself to invest no energy toward joy robbers; instead, nurture the friend treasures. One of my favorite Irish quotes expresses what a true friend would wish for you, "May you live as long as you want, and may you never want as long as you live." Another favorite expresses the priceless treasure of true friendship, "A joy shared is doubled, a sorrow cut in half."

Daily Joy Reflection

What am I looking forward to?

In Summary

Intuition is the faculty of your soul. Joy is the protective attribute of your soul. The Ancient Secrets are right here, hidden in your spine and brain, and as near as your breath. Your breathing is informing you. As you bravely face challenges, fortifying your Soul Wall, saturating your inner atmosphere with radiant light and calmness, know that you are blazing the trails of collective consciousness. This is a service to self and all of mankind. You are contributing from the joy you access, the purity of prana that flows into and through your spine and brain. This is the most powerful gift to give yourself and others in mankind's loony-bin creation. With each lesson learned, continue to bless, release, and give thanks for all who played their roles in motivating you to connect to and fully embody fierce joy.

Remember to celebrate every little step into continuity of calmness, fun, and increasing tenderness. Be like the baby who is still connected to Joy Source prior to all the fear conditioning. The baby is purehearted and bold in their eagerness to explore. At every challenge, babies will repeat their efforts to roll over, to sit up, to stand, to walk, to run. They may cry when they fall, but they never judge themselves. Like the bold purehearted baby, be determined to get back up on your feet, and stay up. Keep going, facing whatever is in front of you with curiosity. With each beautiful lesson, you'll learn to accept advances and setbacks as normal, to be dealt with as they arise. As a practicing master of the Ancient Secrets, you'll begin to take it all in stride and roar with fierce joy.

EMBODIED JOY IS THE EXPERIENCE OF GOD

Made in the USA
Las Vegas, NV
23 July 2024

92803162R00089